MW01109058

THE
QUEST
FOR
SPIRITURAL
TRUTH

By Randal S. Kinkade

Printed in the United States of America

ISBN 978-1-60266-828-7

www.xulonpress.com

This book is dedicated to Jerry who pushed me,
kicking and screaming, down my path.

And to Jeshua who met me there.

THE QUEST FOR SPIRITUAL TRUTH

PREFACE

In contemplating spiritual truth a lot comes into play. There are numerous belief worldviews and they have countless variations. These worldviews have doctrines that sometimes complement and often contradict each other. How can we know what is true and what is not? That is a tough question. This book may not completely answer that question for you but it will unfold a process that has helped others move down that path.

The title of this book contains the word "Truth". This is a definitive word and requires that we establish whether or not truth exists, and if it does how do we determine what the truth really is? By looking at the last sentence you may surmise that I believe that truth does exist. There are those who would argue that idea. Many stand by the premise that absolute truth does not exist; that all is relative and we, in some fashion, create our own truths.

The short argument to the statement "There is no such thing as absolute truth" is "is that absolutely true?" It is my intent to use logic, math and science in a hunt for spiritual truth, and to see if we should even assume an absolute spiritual truth.

I could write what I believe, state that it is true and give you the reasons why I believe it is so, but that type of book has been done many times before. If many worldviews have contradictory philosophies, writing my worldview and claiming it as the truth is of no help. What follows is an anecdotal process for asking some definitive and sometimes hard questions of your worldview and belief systems and a scientific process for you to seek honest answers.

We are creatures with a mind that reasons. Before we accept any spiritual belief we need to build a foundation that satisfies that mind. Conversely we must also use that same level of reason when accepting something as false.

How do we do that? We need to turn up the evidence that supports our spiritual hypothesis. This has to be provable, solid evidence. We must be willing to show a modicum of faith to allow for some of the intangibles, but by and large we need enough evidence to give that faith a solid footing.

For example, will the sun come up tomorrow? The most common answer, in the middle latitudes, is yes. How could someone assume that? Because ever since we have been aware of such things the sun has risen daily. Does that mean there is no possibility that tomorrow it will fail? Of course not. But the odds are in our favor that the sun will repeat its on-going trend. We may not know with the absolute certainty we have that 2+2=4, but we can have faith based on our current evidence.

My belief is that the process of logical thought will lead us to the truth. In the following pages we will use logic and science to explore truth, presupposition, following spiritual rules and so on. The intent is to help us think about our belief systems, and the others around us, more completely.

I believe spiritual truth exists and throughout the pages of this book you will see the process I have used to come to that end. I think it is important to say that what I believe isn't the issue. What is important is what you believe and how you have come to your belief. It is my hope this book will help you decide if what you believe holds up to the elements of scientific and evidential fact.

Everyone has a worldview that they use to make decisions. No matter if you are inclined toward the spiritual or the atheistic the process of working through the answers to the questions posed in this book will do one of two things for you. It will either confirm your faith in the system you now hold to or it will offer up questions that you haven't asked or have yet to fully answer. Either way it serves a purpose in a process. Being sure is a satisfying thing.

If you enter the process with an open heart, an open mind and with tough skin, you stand a wonderful chance of establishing a solid faith based on evidence and not just on feelings or the family history of such beliefs. This book will not answer all of the questions that will arise in such a quest but it will offer a point of departure and lead to other sources that will help you continue if you need to. It is my hope that you enjoy the journey and that the journey satisfies your reasoning mind.

1.

PRESUPPOSITION

What color is a blackberry when it's green? Already you have either an answer formulated or a procedure in motion to get an answer acceptable to your thinking process. There are four common, possible starting points.

1) There are those who truly believe that they know the answer but still have it wrong.

2) There are those who don't know, and know they don't know, but have surmised an answer that they will stick with all the same.

3) There are those who believe they don't yet have enough information to answer confidently.

4) There are those who know the answer, without a doubt, because of past research and experience.

Before we move on, determine where you were on the above list right after you read the question.

Everyone has a tendency to go into situations with presuppositions, an already established way of reacting to a question or event. This process opens the possibility of leading us down a wrong path at times. For the question above, for instance, if you presuppose that green is only a color you will be lead to a certain answer. If you presuppose that green defines the state of unripe fruit then the answer may or may not be different. Presuppositions often are not based on fact but on interpretation of gathered information. That gathered information may not be complete or may have been tainted by inaccurate data. If the information seemed reasonable at the time we will log it as "factual" and continue from there. The trouble arises when we close our mind to interpretations that don't fit in with our "factual" database.

So how do you find the answer to this question? I could just give you the answer, in fact, I feel obligated to do so because I posed the question in the first place to make my point. The thought you should have (according to my presupposition of such things) is, "How can I trust his answer?"

The only way I know is to research and observe the situation with an open mind. First you will need to learn how to properly identify a blackberry plant. A little research at the library or seeking out a naturalist familiar with such things should do the trick. Then go to an area where they grow and observe them early in the season before the fruit is ripe.

You see now from the last line that I have defined "green", at the very least, as being pre-ripened fruit. (Unless you already knew the answer, you now have more information then when you started. Has your answer changed?)

The answer I have comes originally from a saying taught to me by a park ranger mentor named Ed. He thought that at 3 O'clock in the morning toward the end of a long night shift that the saying was hilarious.

"Randy", he'd say. "Did you know that a black-berry is red when it's green?"

I always chuckled when he'd say that, partially because at 3 a.m. a lot of things are funny, partially because as the senior law enforcement officer Ed carried a gun. The saying was catchy and presented by someone I trusted so I accepted it as true. But one spring, wanting to back up the saying with evidence, I went to the edge of a field that had blackberry plants and looked for myself. By golly if ol' Ed wasn't right!

We can't enter into a situation without presup-position. We all have experience, ideas and interpre-tations developed because of our worldview. This worldview leads us to presuppose certain things and affects our beliefs. (We will explore the possibility that belief does not necessarily equal truth in the next chapter.) The question is how do we optimize the gathering of information to be open to actual truth?

One evening at dinner my 8 year old son said, "A daddy long-leg has a poison more powerful than a Black Widow, but we don't have to worry because its fangs are too short to bite people." I had heard the assertion before when I was a hiking guide so I asked how he knew this to be true. "My teacher told me today." His presupposition at 8 years old was that the teacher would not tell him a lie so it must be so. I told him I didn't believe it was true but my wife, Susan, took his side. During the ensuing discussion he and she bolstered each other. Sam believed it because the teacher wouldn't lie and because he believed that all the support he needed was another authority figure to corroborate his point of view. Susan provided that.

I asked my wife why she believed it to be true and her answer was just as nebulous. She said, "Someone at work told me they saw it on the Web." I went on to say that logically it didn't make sense, because a daddy long-leg wasn't even a spider from what I had heard. The fact was that I had no more definitive evidence to prove my point than they had to prove theirs. So we set out on a quest. My wife and I went to work to research the question with some guidelines. She could look up the information on the web but the authors of the articles she selected had to be proven experts in the field. Any research that I brought back had to have the same merit. A few days later we reconvened and shared what we had found. The result of the search and the resulting reactions show another human aspect that allows us to keep hanging on to a particular point of view. We hate to be wrong!

I went to the dictionary and found, according to Webster's that the daddy long-leg was an insect, so I used that to taunt my wife. I then chose to go to the experts at the Arizona-Sonora Desert Museum Entomology Department, near our home in Tucson, to see what they had to say. My wife went back to a broad search on the Web. Susan's research was done before mine and she made her presentation.

Her attack started with the comment, "you were wrong. They are not insects and they do have 8 legs." She proceeded to give me the details of why what I had claimed was incorrect but she left out the details that would show where she had gone astray. That approach is often used when we want to cling to our point of view. The things we hear that builds on our presupposition are readily taken in, often without further research. Anything contrary to our presupposition is brushed off as not likely, no matter what the qualifications of the person who puts forth the information.

When Susan was done taking out her joy at my misinformation she had to hand over the printed document that established that I was wrong. The whole story showed that there was a possibility of two creatures being called daddy-longlegs. Both are in the animal class Arachnida, but one is in the order Opiliones, and therefore not a true spider. (So Webster's was wrong in calling it an insect but I can be partially vindicated in that it is not a spider either.) So the first creature is typically a scavenger that makes its living eating decomposing plants and animals. It has neither venom glands nor fangs. The article also states that most people don't even see these guys because they hang out under rocks and logs. This is a statement that I would have to disagree with because the creature described in the article is the one I saw often walking through the lawns of my childhood. So even as the logic of the original argument takes hold in my mind I am reminded that all facts need to be double checked. (See Chapter two). The other creature is a true spider, but because there is no reference to this type of spider biting a human and causing serious damage the claim cannot be substantiated. The article points out that if these were deadly and their fangs weren't long enough to inject the poison in humans we could only find this out by "milking" one and then injecting the venom into a human or similar creature to see how it reacts with the test subject. Since this experiment has never been documented the supposition can not be proven to be true and therefore we can safely determine that the original statement is a myth.

The important part of this exercise ultimately was not who was right and who was wrong but what the actual facts are in the case. Once we have researched the truth we can know that when we talk about this subject in the future we both will be right. It is that sort of open-mindedness that needs to be in place to overcome strong presuppositions, even if the outcome causes a great change in your worldview.

Mindfulness, or awareness, is an important element when looking for those answers. Mindfulness is to simply be aware of what is going on around you while it is going on or to be aware of what you are doing when you are doing it. The trick for us is to limit the filter of our presupposition so that we can analyze the presented information with an open heart and mind.

I once worked at a resort that taught "mindfulness based stress reduction". The trouble was that some of the teachers would properly teach the concept of being mindful of others and of being open minded but in their lives open-mindedness was defined thusly: "You are open minded as long as you agree with my point of view and don't require me to really consider your point of view." This sort of person has the belief that we all should be open-minded but they become closed minded to your point of view if you don't agree with them. Their presupposition leads them to believe that since they put time and effort into the process of arriving at this conclusion, the work is already done and anything you have to offer is unnecessary.

The win-win situation, in this type of case, is when you compromise until my needs are met, no matter the cost to you. If I "win" and I perceive your compromise as nominal, no matter how you perceive it, I can comfortably go home believing we have a win-win situation and I can feel good about it. To me this is a classic example of not having an open mind or heart. And when we endeavor to seek "The Truth" we have to remain truly open minded, even when some of the answers don't yet fit into our worldview.

I equate someone lost in their quest for spiritual truth to a drowning person. In the panic of knowing that they might die in the water anything presenting itself as something that will keep them afloat will be grabbed and used to prevent that end. This is true even if the object might hurt them. The possibility of saving their own life will rule out the fact that what was thrown to them was something that may actually cause them harm. Even if the object can help they may use it poorly and cause themselves more harm than good. In such times it is hard to remain calm and open-minded. A second swimmer, who makes their way out to assist the drowning swimmer has to be cautious. Even though they have come to save the one in trouble, both may drown if panic occurs and the rescuer isn't prepared for the fight that may be put up by the person seeking help. At this stage calm words and logic won't convince the troubled swimmer to just lay back and trust the rescuer. Only an open mind will allow the swimmer to be saved.

There are spiritual leaders, in all worldviews, with poorly thought out or poorly interpreted ideas, doing the equivalent of throwing cement blocks to drowning swimmers. And sadly I see the people flocking to grab the cement blocks.

Consider this problem of spiritual darkness, defined as an area of uncertainty. If you wanted out of an area of unknowing, of darkness, anything presenting itself to you in a way that fits your worldview would be a light shining in that darkness; truthful or not, logical or not, good for you or not.

To use an extreme example, consider being lost deep within the earth in a cave. Your objective would be to find a way out and to be bathed by the light of the sun and to be able to see the clear blue sky. In the cave there is no light, no use of your vision, only blackness. The chance of finding your way safely through the corridors of the cave would be increased greatly with any form of light. If it were completely dark and a form of light presented itself you would make use of it.

Having that light, however, doesn't guarantee that you will find your way out of the cave. You will need proper directions along with that light to assure proper passage. Without proper instruction you may still wander forever lost but now with the ability to see the walls that contain you. You may even come to find comfort in those walls and your artificial light source forgetting that what you really desire is the sun and the clear blue sky. You may not be reminded of that desire until your artificial light source fails.

I've seen this sort of thing in my spiritual quest. I've seen it in other peoples quests as well. We wander saying that we want the truth, knowing that we had already determined the parameters within which we would allow for that truth to exist. I, and many others, look for religions that allow us to do as we please and offer the hope that we are doing a truly right thing. The trouble, I found, was that when the hard questions were asked I didn't have sufficient answers so I ignored the trouble spots and focused on how the stuff I liked made me feel so good and right. Being an outdoor kind of guy I sought things that not only made me feel good but that kept me in the woods. I found that anything that did that was accepted by me without much analysis. If it allowed me to get away with things less than morally acceptable, all the better. If someone brought to me a worldview that would take me away from these things it was easy to criticize it and not listen with the aforementioned open mind.

So I set up a presupposition that only allowed for the things I wanted to be a part of my religion and if the things presented to me by others were in opposition to that I easily discounted them. If I was told that I couldn't seek God in the woods or that the rocks and the plants of the earth didn't have a spirit or that I was wrong for allowing my animal nature to be satisfied any way it called then I was critical of their intervention. That sort of thought process is common with people on this quest. The question is, does that allow for the possibility of truth to penetrate the shell of our wants in this subject?

Back to the light example. Let's say that it is dark in your room and you want to read. Without light you can't see to read so you seek out a light source. You find a small night light and plug it into the wall socket across the room from your reading chair. You now have enough light to see something of the room so you can make it safely back to your chair. Sitting in your chair in the opposite corner of your room the light doesn't help you to read. So you take a pillow and a blanket over to the night light and sit on the floor. Not an ideal situation but it is all you have so you make it work. When you get uncomfortable sitting on the floor you decide to find a better light source. A 40 watt bulb for your bedside lamp is located in your bedside table drawer so you replace the old bulb and your view of the room gets noticeably better. You can now lie on your bed and see well enough to read and you can see the room much better. The contrast between the small night light and the 40 watt bulb is noticeable enough that you may not even consider searching for more.

As your eyes get tired from reading with the 40 watt bulb, though, you start to think about how if there was an improvement from light source one to light source two there just may be something more. That is this quest.

If we take a serious look at world religions we will see common ground. Light exists in all of them even the ones in which we disagree. What we need to do is to not stop just because we have a 40 watt light source but be sure that a 150 watt light doesn't exist as well. We may be able to get by with a dim light but we can see much more clearly with the benefit of full illumination. If you were reading by the night light and someone turned on the overhead 150 watt bulb the night light would become inconsequential. It is a good idea to wander through the house to see what other light source there are. If we can quell our presupposition we can see more objectively which light source is best.

We often build our suppositions by saying "if" this "then" that. For example, if there is such a thing as gravity, then when I let go of the rock I am holding it will fall to the ground. If gravity, then a fall.

I can create any sort of theory I choose based on this configuration but if my first IF, THEN is faulty then so too will be all the others stacked on top of it. (IF my first is wrong, THEN so is the rest of my argument.)

With my presupposition at work before I make my first IF, THEN I am more likely to allow for a faulty first configuration. IF I want a certain outcome, THEN I will set up the foundational configuration accordingly to assure that the outcome will match my presupposition.

Hypothesis builds on hypothesis: If the first is wrong the equation built by the whole chain will be wrong. If you went to the store and bought a can of peaches, brought them home, opened them, poured them into a bowl but what came out was cinnamon apples what would you infer about the situation? An evolutionist may surmise that matter reacted with matter in the can and the peaches evolved into apples; The highly spiritual might surmise that God realized your need for the nutrients found in the apples so He metaphysically changed the product for your well-being; the pragmatist may say the folks at the processing plant messed up and mislabeled the can.

From the point of view of the three belief systems listed we can come up with an argument that makes sense to each individual's way of thinking. Once locked into, no matter how far off it seems to someone else, we will rationalize our point of view as being the correct one.

For instance, take the evolution point of view. Over eons of time matter has reacted with matter countless times to change and produce new and varied species. Therefore, within the sealed and pressurized confines of the can, matter may have had a perfect environment to effect the evolutionary change from peach to apple.

The Theistic point of view. God is all powerful and all knowing. If He knew that I needed the vitamins of the apple instead of the peach he has the power, knowledge and authority to cause a change in the very can I brought home to assure me of proper nutrition. It was obviously divine intervention.

The pragmatic point of view. People and machines are fallible. Those knot-heads at the plant missed a label notation on their computer and started the cans of apples before they cancelled the peach labels. Now I can't have my favorite peach dessert unless I go back to the store.

The trouble is no matter what our opinion, from the point of view of each perspective the story they lay out can be proven to their satisfaction with their presuppositions. What someone from outside of these presuppositions must do is to do the research and see if any of these perspectives fit with the facts of the matter. (See Chapter Two) But where do we begin?

Logic dictates that we start at the easiest point. This may be to prove or disprove the simplest supposition. In this case we go to the canning factory to see if the line manager has discovered any errors in the production line procedures. If we find that, yes the label procedure messed up and we know that they put the wrong labels on the apples, and then we can be reasonably assured that nothing bigger has gone on. Or can we? This discovery may still be argued from certain perspectives. The theist may still say "Sure the label guy messed up but why? Could it be that I was still to get apples instead of my desired peaches and God orchestrated the mistake? Certainly not an impossibility from that perspective. It does seem to rule out the evolutionist perspective. He may not have any reason to disbelieve the truth of his worldview but it can be reasoned, that at least in this instance, a transmutation didn't occur.

So in this scenario we will rule out option one and still consider the other two. Which is most likely? I think the pragmatist's perspective is the most likely. The report from the line manager fits well and he can tell us exactly when the problem started, when it was corrected and how many cans were mislabeled. Even the theist would have to say that the possibility of it happening that way is possible and even probable in the natural world. The presupposition of the theist, in this case, can't be completely shut down but I feel most would rule it out. Even other theists. It is still possible, however, that from the theists perspective, an all knowing all powerful God could have caused the event for purposes beyond our comprehension. How do we find what is true?

We can be certain that the cans were mislabeled. We can't be 100 percent certain that there wasn't an outside source for that outcome. In such a case it may make sense for us to combine the two. A pragmatic theist might just say, "Hey. I got apples instead of peaches. I can cover my bets by making apple crisp instead of peach cobbler." (Now if in preparation of your topping you open up the oatmeal container and find a pie crust...)

We can not effectively go through this process without being in a state of true awareness. It is easy to get to a certain stage and then relax in the comfort that we have arrived. This will lead to complacency. In that state it is easy to develop a crust that grows harder and harder to penetrate with new and some-times critical information.

When I was a hiking guide I would urge people to become more aware of their surroundings when we were on the trail. The people who complied were the ones who felt they could use the information we taught them on the trail and apply it to their lives when they were away from the hike. Many of these folks were from the city and this nature stuff was only a diversion during a vacation. What was important was the information they could take back to their real world. I often couched the improvisational lessons in such a way as to help them realize that the lesson could go home with them.

One of the things the hiking guides stressed was "awareness." Too many of the hikers were oblivious to what was going on around them. We encouraged them to notice how the hills affected their breath and muscles, how the elements of nature tended to be more subtle and how to see more of what was presented there. We would often leave in the light of dawn but before the sun would rise over the moun-tains. We would hike up the first several hills then stop for a short water break. At that break I would face the crowd with my back to the east. During the break I would talk about the desert and answer ques-tions from the guests. At a certain point I would raise my hand and point over my shoulder and say "ladies and gentlemen, I give you sunrise!"

At that exact moment the sun would crest the mountains behind me and illuminate the awestruck guests. They would ooh and aah at the beautiful sight then they would express amazement at my unique talent. Because the resort had a focus on spiritual awakening, some believed that I had some sort of metaphysical gift, some, the pragmatists, thought I got lucky and would not be able to repeat the trick. The open-minded folks didn't presuppose but asked me, "How'd you do that?"

The fact is with experience on that trail and awareness of the natural world it is a given that anyone could do the same. It has been known for centuries that the sun rises in the east and the time and location on the horizon changes from day to day and season to season. I am certain there must be a mathematical formula that satisfies the explanation for what I did. I'm not smart enough to figure out that formula. I am smart enough to know that if I use my awareness of the shortening shadows of the mountains behind me I can precisely predict when the sun will crest. I will also, with practice and awareness, be able to figure out that the actual time of the cresting will change from day to day and season to season. No magic. No metaphysics, just paying attention and being aware.

When someone in the group would ask I always told them candidly of my "secret". That opened the conversation so I could encourage them to sharpen their awareness in ways that made sense to them. It can be argued that I have the ability I have because of God given traits or that I evolved such abilities, but the pragmatist would say anyone, with an interest, could do the same. Even if we could make an argument for the other two, the pragmatic point of view is definitively true.

Our awareness needs to be honed no matter where it comes from. We have to be aware of what we believe and why we believe it. (I think that if there is an ultimate creator-God, that God must have given us a way to discern this sort of thing even when the full answer is not apparent to the naked eye). We also have to be aware of what it means and how other information from outside sources affects our beliefs. We must be aware enough to be able to effectively explain the how's and why's of our spiritual beliefs and be open enough to hear other perspectives, apply those thoughts and then be able to prove or disprove those theories in light of the factual base we have. Awareness is critical in knowing what our beliefs are and to be able to logically counter another's perspective, and even ours, if it doesn't hold up to reasonable proof. The ultimate goal of this quest is not in conforming the world to our truth, but in conforming our world to The Truth.

2.

WHAT IS TRUTH?

The short answer to the question "what is truth?" is that the truth is the truth no matter what we believe. It is said that there are many paths to achieving the truth. Does it matter what path we use to get there?

It is easy to turn pure white, a definite truth, into gray with rationalization. I do it all of the time. I inject my hopes and desires into a definite truth to make it fit my wants or perceived needs thus diluting the truth. Any truth can be distorted to fit our needs. Let's explore the statement "the sky is blue". Most would agree but I don't. Allow me my attempt at distortion.

Certainly I see blue most of the time because I live in the desert. But what about clouds? They are white, gray, and during a great thunderstorm even purple. So the sky isn't "blue" it is multi-colored.

"Clouds are clouds", you say? Yes, but where do they reside? In the sky. As part of the sky they have to be considered and therefore the sky is not blue, it has many colors.

Not convinced? Let me use science. The things that we see with our eyes are the result of what is reflected. From the sky we see the blue part of the spectrum that reflects back to us. All of the colors we don't see are the parts of the spectrum that are absorbed. Think about it. The reflected aspect is not within the element. The character of any element is all that is within, or what has been absorbed. Therefore the sky is every color *but* blue!

Now let's go back to the beginning. The truth is the truth no matter what we believe. I know there are those who could be convinced by the previous arguments. But, if I believe it and you are convinced does that make it true? As we gather information on any subject we develop our opinions. As more information comes in we add to or subtract from those things we consider to be the truth. My suggestion is that we make our judgments but remain open to potential change. If you believe the sky is blue hold to that, listen to my counter offer openly, apply the information that you can verify with whatever tools you have, disprove with openness what you can, reassess your stand then go forward prepared to repeat the process. At some point you will come to the realization that you have logically and scientifically explored the options and no one has brought you any new, pertinent information that can change your mind. That is your truth.

With a diligent enough search your truth and The Truth will coincide. Keep searching, though, because the truth is the truth no matter what we believe.

When I was ten years old I had a friend named Carl. It seemed that we were always at odds about what was the best when it came to things that we really weren't old enough to know about. We had our opinions none the less. One day while playing with our cars I said that the best cars were made by Ford. Carl disagreed; Chevrolet was the best in his mind. Wanting to be able to get along I then offered up that surely he'd agree that in the world of motorcycles Honda was top notch. Nope, it had to be Harley Davidson. With tractors he liked Farmall and I liked John Deere.

I see this sort of division in the world much of the time. Is it Coke or Pepsi, Ford or Chevy, Republican or Democrat? We polarize with the top names without much thought of the gray elements. Why don't the masses think about R.C. Cola or Pontiac or the Libertarian party?

If you react as I did as a child your opinions may come from the people around you who influence you. I didn't really know the difference between Ford and Chevy other than the way they looked and what the adults around me said. The thing that concerns me is that many continue with the opinions of their youth without ever doing research or putting their opinion to the test.

In the world of gray it must be noted that black and white do exist. (In fact it is the mixture of black with white that creates gray). In our secular world we see everyday that folks get pretty worked up over "my black versus your white".

So we tend to avoid gray in such things in general until it comes to religion. At that topic it seems that gray is the route people choose and those who go with a black or white stance are criticized or ridiculed. (In a chapter 8 we will explore spiritual camouflage but if the gods we choose have an everlasting effect isn't it strange that on this topic we all of a sudden walk into an area of fog, forsaking our secular tendency to draw the line on a black and white stand?)

Again the black and white stand holds strong until we come to the topic of religion. Of course there are certainly those who are convinced that the way they follow is the only way. As I began my search into this realm, I realized how much tolerance there was for the use of gray and how much objection there was for particular black and white views. Try this experiment sometime. Ask people at a gathering what spiritual practice they subscribe to and then watch the reactions of the others in the room as the answers are put forth. I have noticed that the grayer the practice the more easily accepted it is. As with all things there are exceptions to this. If someone in the room has a solid Black or White stance they will make it known and then the ones in gray tend to solidify the fact that gray is better thus turning their stance into one resembling black or white.

It is interesting to note that it is expected we will polarize on secular things; having great competitions over who is right and who is wrong; or finding great camaraderie in being with those who agree with our stance. I see car window stickers with a kid urinating on the opposing team or product logo, and bumper stickers like "I'd rather eat worms that drive a Ford". To me, because of the prevalence, it seems that we have a designed instinct to define things in simple black or white ways no matter how uncouth the methods. I do it, you do it, and they do it, so my brain, trained in law enforcement, starts to wonder why? Why, when a topic as potentially important as spiritual belief comes along, do we wander into a world of gray?

The danger lies in not exploring more. We all have opinions that come from our worldview. We all have presuppositions. But to be sure that what we believe is the truth we need to keep an open mind around our worldview and presuppositions and take in more information. If my reason for liking Fords is because we had them when I was a kid and my stepfather said they were the best, I need to do more research to be sure that my opinion is based on more that just parroting what I heard around me growing up. I need to not only drive my own Ford but I need to see what is offered by Chevy, Pontiac and Mercedes before I proclaim a true allegiance.

Now, I may decide that Mercedes is better but I can't afford one. In the secular world we can settle for that. "Boy, I'd love to have one of those but it cost too much" is common for us. When we get to the spiritual world, though, what is the consequence of settling? Early in the discussion I think it is easy for us to say that there is none, but the deeper one goes the more that will change. Ultimately in the car world these things are probably not critical. Any new or properly maintained car will get me safely from point A to point B. The question that needs answering from this book is "does knowledge and understanding of spiritual truth have a more lasting consequence than what brand of car I drive or whose beverage I drink?"

If you are paying attention you may have surmised that I think that the answer is yes. You may also have pondered whether I might have a black or white stance on the matter. It is safe to assume so. But I believe it is of greater importance that you have and take the opportunity to explore further your stance. If reincarnation is a fact you need to do things well so that you progress properly: if resurrection is correct, you need to know that and decide accordingly; if we die and just turn to dust, what do you want to do with your life now? We all do what we do based on such a worldview. The question is which of these world-views, if any, is based on The Truth?

(I know, that statement surmises one truth. So let's see if logic and science leads us to one truth or if it leads us to the possibility of many truths.)

Keep in mind that we can be on the same journey but gather and interpret basic information substantially differently. A few years back I took a trip on the Green river in Utah with two friends. When we returned from the trip we heard the story of a couple, one of which had done this trip before, who got all of the information they needed to do the trip well but paddled into trouble none the less.

36

They started the day after we did with the intention of being picked up by the outfitters at the same place and on the same day as us. This meant they would have to paddle a bit harder to make it but the outfitter allowed the schedule because they knew the couple had enough time. The details were explained and they chose that option.

Unknowingly we saw them on the river on our second day. They blasted past us with full, passionate strokes and seemed very focused on not slowing down. We thought they were trying to get to a prized campsite before it was taken. We were lounging as they passed, with our paddles stowed and we joked with them "Oh, that's what those things are for!" They agreed that we were probably doing it right but kept right on going and were soon out of sight. At that point we just wondered which campsite we wouldn't get because of their dedication.

We were on the same river encountering the same current, curves, scenery and weather but their focus was substantially different. We all have our worldview and perspective which gives us our ideas on what we need to do to get by. They believed that they were behind schedule and were not going to be at the rendezvous point on time. We were friendly as they passed and enveloped in the same circumstance but they didn't even attempt to gather more information from us. Even if they were embarrassed about their situation a casual "when are you folks being picked up?" or "what canyon is that?" would have helped them establish where they were and what they needed to do to make their schedule. They may not even have thought themselves in trouble but that ignorance was to show itself to be not so blissful later in their trip. The Truth: once they caught up with us they had as much time as we did to make the pick up spot. At that point they could have eased up and stowed their paddles too.

Witnesses later reported that the wife said she was an outdoor educator at a school and had worked for many years as a canoe guide in the Boundary Waters Canoe Area in northern Minnesota and, as mentioned before, had done this trip previously. The owner of the outfitting company said with all of that they sounded like the ideal customer. So even with substantial background in the sport at hand things began to fall apart.

The trip we chose is a 55 mile float from drop off to pick up. We planned on a 4 night, 5 day trip. They had 3 nights and 4 days. They made 30 miles the first day on a river that has an average current of 4 miles per hour. (By contrast we did only 14 miles on our first day).

If we use the river as a metaphor they were on the same quest as my friends and I, they had received the same information on how to proceed safely, but their point of view was so much different.

The outfitter does a great job of marking up your map with landmarks, campsites and points of interest along the way. According to the outfitter, this couple had the regular places noted such as the light class two water at Millard Canyon. In river running rapids are rated from 1 to 6. A 1 is very easy to run and a 6 is deadly. Approaching Millard Canyon on the river it makes itself known when you are ¼ mile away sounding like a class 4 rapids. It was reported that when they got there they grumbled that the spot hadn't been noted by the outfitter and they wondered why. This comes back to haunt them later.

Three miles beyond Millard Canyon is Anderson Bottom. It is an abandoned meander, a place where the river once made a long loop but erosion ate away at the river walls and the water cut through to shorten its route by two and a half miles. This landmark comes back at our couple as well. The river hasn't followed the route of the meander for a long time and on the map the old route is noted with a lighter blue line than the blue that shows the actual current river channel. Thinking they were still far above this point they continued to paddle hard to make the pick up point on time.

A day before their scheduled pick up they pass what they believe to be Anderson Bottom. It is actually the confluence with the Colorado River. They had unknowingly passed Anderson bottom 31 miles up stream. A mile and a half later they pass a sign that warns that Cataract Canyon and its class 5 white water rapids is 2.5 miles away, life jackets are now required and don't attempt to go beyond Spanish Bottom without the appropriate white water gear. The sign, the husband believed, had been vandalized and the white water was still 22.5 miles away. Two and a quarter miles later, still paddling hard, they hear the rapids and believe them to be the promised announcement of the class two riffle of Millard Canyon. Remember, they had already passed what they believed to be Anderson Bottom which, according to the map, was three miles below Millard. Another major piece of evidence missed.

So, they unexpectedly hit serious white water paddling hard, in a full, open canoe without life jackets because they were told the Green River was a flat water route. In fact it is, but they were now on the Colorado River. The good news is that all they lost was their boat, all their gear except the river toilet (who says there ain't a God?), and their credit cards. When they emerged, one on each side of the river, they decided to walk downstream because they still believed they were several miles upstream on the Green River.

I want to be fair to the couple as best I can. I never got the chance to interview them after the event. As an outdoor guide though, and one who is comfortable teaching people about nature as the wife claimed to be, I can't see how all the clues didn't add up for them. Even if nothing else registered, as they paddled into Cataract Canyon, there should have been a wake up call that the other things that they believed in were not holding water. (Pardon the pun).

The route is established for any who choose to take the journey. The map is filled with the details and the landmarks remain constant. Even if you miss call a canyon or two the other details are numerous so you can correct yourself soon enough. Ignoring Millard Canyon, misunderstanding an abandoned meander, misinterpreting the confluence and doubting an explicit sign all point to tunnel vision. This condition states "I am right and no amount of truth can sway that".

This information from a metaphoric journey becomes a very pertinent point in our quest. The rulebook, the map that we follow, should remain unchanging and explicit. (See Chapter Three.) We run into trouble, like the rapids, when we add, subtract, ignore, disbelieve or fail to ask for informed help when seeking the details of the truth. One in that situation will take the rules they like and be dogmatic about following them but will ignore other rules because they don't agree with them.

The truth is the truth no matter what we believe. The end result (Maybe Cataract Canyon) awaits us no matter if we know that it's coming, ignore the possibility or just misread the map.

If we refer to the truth as being pure white and falsehood as being absolutely black how do we effectively filter out the gray? We run into trouble when we realize that my truth and your truth don't correlate. What I "know" to be true based on my evidence could be quite different than what you "know" to be true based on your evidence.

Absolute truth is defined by Norman Geisler in "The Nature of Truth", as "truth for everyone, everywhere, at all times." He also suggests that "All truth is absolute". The thing to keep in mind is that in matters of Absolute Truth, and if truth exists so must its perfect form, we could both be wrong which places us smack dab into the world of gray.

There is the belief among some that there is no such thing as absolute truth. This premise allows that you can believe what you believe and I can believe what I believe and we will both be in the absolutely white category. There is a logical problem with that thought process. We can prove that truth exists by a study in contrast. (See chapter 4) Even to be able to use the word truth presupposes the concept of falsehood. It is fair to say that we can have different opinions on a subject but in the matter of absolute truth we have to know that only those who follow those things defined as absolute truth will be completely correct. I can chose not to follow but ultimately I have to concede that the truth is the truth. If we want to believe that it is all right for you and I to have opposing points of view and have them both viewed as being accept-able we have to hope that your world and mine won't overlap. If you say that rape is wrong and I say that it is all right I would assume that you will hope that I never cross into your world with my worldview.

We also need to look at the thought process of the world at large. What do the majority of people who reside in different cultures say about the question? If you do a study of this you will see that, barring the aberrant most cultures agree on certain moral truths. One who doesn't want any absolutes might say it is OK for me to think rape is acceptable but I suppose that man would not let me be alone with his wife or daughter.

It is easy to proclaim "truths" in theory when trying to make a point on how you want to be left alone to do what you want to do. Those theories, without foundations in logic and science, come crashing down in the face of harsh reality.

As you look into different cultures and different ages you will find that there is abundant correlation in what people believe to be true morally and spiritually. Differences in details will be obvious but so to will be similarities in foundational beliefs. These include such things as a God or gods exist, stealing is wrong, I must leave your spouse alone, it is right to be respectful and loving to others, it is all right to protect yourself and your family even when it breaks some of the above rules (but only defensively, never offensively), and so on.

These universal agreements point to a foundation that has been set out by someone or something bigger than us humans. It indicates that those foundational basics are established and required by that someone and over the centuries we have added to or subtracted from those requirements.

So much overlap from nation to nation shows a common starting point. Wouldn't it be satisfying to uncover the original truths to see where we began to add or subtract to fit our comfort level as a culture?

The trouble is that if you do the research into the various religious beliefs to discover the above you will also notice something else. There are numerous belief systems out there that often conflict with each other but which also claim to be the truth. It has come to the point that it is acceptable to say that you and I believe different things, they are contrary to one another but we can call them both "The Truth" because not to do so would cause disharmony. That theory doesn't fit if we stay with the premise of this chapter. The truth is the truth no matter what we believe and that means that if you and I disagree on conflicting elements of our worldview there are only three choices: you are right and I am wrong, I am right and you are wrong, or we both are wrong.

The frustration for me had always been how to know for certain, when everyone else seemed so certain. Logic dictates that 2+2 cannot have two different answers yet that's what a quest for any kind of truth tends to uncover. If there are several answers given for one solid question there must be some that are mistaken or at best some that are only partial truths. How can we know for sure?

My suggestion is to engage in this quest with conviction. You believe something at this point. Keep an open mind and gather more information. Be sure the information comes from more than just someone's feelings on a subject and check to see if it can be defined logically. As mentioned in the preface there are things that will require us to believe in something unseen but there still needs to be enough evidence in that faith to make it reasonable.

To do that we must define and interpret the rules of our worldview.

3.

PLAYING BY THE RULES

When I was a kid I played the game Monopoly with a friend who enacted a rule I had never heard of before. He said that whenever a tax is paid the money is put into the center of the board and whenever a person lands on the "Free Parking" space they collect all the money in the pot. That bothered me because it wasn't in the rulebook. Over the years I found that many people use this rule. It has become a grassroots method of play. I'm still not convinced that it's right. Just because it has become commonplace does that make it proper? When following these rules I trust the inventor of the game knew what he was doing and "Free Parking" was designated "Free Parking" for a reason

Recently one of my sons received a child's version of Monopoly called "Monopoly Junior". Incorporated in the rules is a version of the above anomaly. The Free Parking space has been replaced by the "Rich Uncle Pennybag's Loose Change" space. The rules state when you land on certain spaces the fee incurred goes to a pile on the loose change space and if you land on there, "you get to take it all!"

In this game it is an official rule so to play properly it must be followed. Every time I play this version with my boys, though, I am reminded of how the rule came about. It is an addition to or subtraction from the foundational rule. If Monopoly were the original truth what has happened is a perfect example of how that perfect truth will be changed by people who want something different. The grassroots movement made the idea for change popular then subsequent versions of the game adopted the new rule. You can see at any game store there are multiple versions of Monopoly. Several of these have rulebooks that change the free parking rule of the original game. If one of these is the first version of the game you played, then you graduate to the original game it may be easy to assume the same sort of rule also applies to the original version. You might not even attempt to check the rulebook because you believe you already know how to play. If others around you play with the made up rule you will never know the difference… unless you check out the rule book.

This is only an annoyance when it happens with a board game. If this is happening with spiritual truth, though, something of value is being compromised.

All major belief systems (world religions) have a rulebook: The Torah for Judaism, The Bible for Christianity, The Qur'an for Islam, The Rig Veda for Hinduism, The Book of Mormon for the Church of Jesus Christ and the Latter Day Saints and so on. In order to fully practice a belief system one must follow the established rules. To knowingly add to or subtract from those rules changes the game and dilutes the system. Consider this: If something is a spiritual truth that truth should remain constant. If a rule is alterable then it can't be from any sort of god it must be equated to a kid changing the rules of Monopoly. God, by definition, is not capricious; He is immutable, unchanging. (Webster's defines God as "the Supreme Being, creator and master of all.") A being with that much authority sets definitive rules. If they change it's because of our interpretation not because He decided he was wrong.

In the United States Christianity is predominate and it has historic examples of this sort of dilution. Things like the Crusades, where armies slaughtered thousands in the name of Christ or TV Evangelists who line their pockets with follower's money by misrepresenting the truth written in their rulebook, cause great rifts in people's ability to believe that the system has merit. If the example of the T. V. evangelist needs to be followed, I don't care to play the game.

No matter what your belief system the essentials of that system must be followed. Christianity states that believing in Christ as God is an essential. Without that you fail to be a Christian. The Bible states a case for God's creation of the universe in accordance with the book of Genesis. Was this universe created in 6 literal days or over millennia? This can be debated but is not an essential to Christian salvation. With the first example non-belief takes you out of the Christian faith, with the second you are just an annoyance to those who believe the other point of view.

As an example of compromising the essentials let's go back to the rules of Monopoly. All players, according to the rules, are to receive $1500 in pre-determined various denominations of bills. When following the essentials is it wrong to receive an additional five $100 bills to replace the prescribed $500 bill? Certainly not. As long as all players start out with the proper amount of cash the essentials are followed. There is still reason for the rule, however. One such reason could be to prevent a shortage at the bank of $100 bills. So to change how the money is sorted is not an essential but will have an effect on the process. Now, once I have my money I personally like to place the bills, long way out, tucked under my side of the board. I place them from lowest to highest denomination from left to right. I do it this way because it is my way of keeping order, and because I watched my older brother do it this way.

Is it essential that you do the same? There is no rule in place to control the way you organize your money. It may make me crazy but you can set up your money opposite of mine, or even just keep it in an unorganized pile. The only essential here is that we all start out with the same amount of cash. How I feel about how you proceed with that cash is my problem. If I decide, as owner of the game board, that you must put your money as I have described under the board, and if you don't you must pay me

$50 each turn until you comply, then I have stepped outside the pale of Monopoly orthodoxy and have altered the rules of the game. If I set that new rule and you agree to its enforcement, that does not make it an official rule of the game. We have strayed from the foundation and anyone who plays by the written rules will not recognize this new rule. If this is the first time you have played the game you may think the rule strange, and you might even comply for the benefit of not having to pay, but how can you know for sure it is the truth?

The solution: Do your homework. If you follow anything blindly you are at the whim of whomever you follow, even if they don't have the intent to mislead. Your responsibility is to check out the leader's actions as it relates to the rulebook. In spiritual practice the same would hold for someone who misinterprets or deliberately changes the meaning of doctrine. Even if they have adherents, that doesn't make it law. The reason we have rulebooks, the Torah, The Bible, The Qur'an, etc. is so we can hold others and be held ourselves accountable. All teaching, actions and beliefs must be tested in light of the rule book.

Here's an example: Have you ever heard the quote "Money is the root of all evil"? As a child I heard this and quoted it but eventually it occurred to me that it didn't quite make sense. Did it mean that all bad things are caused somehow by money? Does that mean that money is bad? I was confused. Later I read that it had been misquoted. That author wrote, "That verse really states 'The love of money is the root of all evil'." That made more sense to me. But... did that mean all of the bad things of the world happened because of greed? Did bad guys rape and murder only for the financial gain? It still didn't follow. It occurred to me to find the quote to see if my sources were correct.

I found that both quotes were wrong. The actual quote contains what the misquotes contain and enough more to have it make sense. The quote is located in the New Testament in the book of First Timothy chapter 6 verse 10, and I quote (but you should double check it) "For the love of money is the root of all kinds of evil." That is something that makes sense even if I don't want to follow it as my truth.

You will find many, like my friend with the "Free Parking" rule, who, when confronted with the fact that their new rule is not found in the original rule-book, will rationalize and assert the new truth needs to exist. They might say, "I know it's not there but it makes so much sense it should be there because it gives us a chance to make even more money." (You may want to counter with "Money is the root of all evil" so that everyone is misusing a rulebook.) If it seems wrong test it, check it, and be sure of it. If at that point you choose to follow the new rule you are doing it by choice with knowledge not ignorance. Keep in mind if you chose to live with it you are also subject to the rewards or consequences of this choice. Be sure you know which outcome you are entitled to with your decision.

As I researched these rules of the original game of Monopoly, I found that my learning of the game had been skewed by my brother's interpretation of the rules. Many things I didn't know are in the rules and many things that we didn't do are required by the rules. I can rationalize by saying "I was young" or "it was just the two of us playing" or even "It was my brother's fault. He was older and didn't pass on all the details that were unnecessary for me to know". Still I am responsible for knowing the rules and I ignorantly and blissfully played the game without double checking those details.

The idea is that no matter what your belief system, you are ultimately responsible for researching the facts. First and foremost does the rulebook you adhere to have the historical and logical truth to back it as a viable plan? Secondly, does the person leading you with that book follow the proper, unadulterated intent of those rules?

If the answer to either of those questions is no, you have some choices to make. The answer lies in whether or not you care to play by the rules.

4.

CONTRAST

Recently, with multiple spiritual leaders and teachers, I have encountered the attitude that things of the spirit are all good and that evil isn't a factor in that world. This concerned me so I began a search as to why I'd be bothered by that attitude. How could I logically determine that evil or "darkness" existed in that realm?

We understand these things due to contrast. We know of black because we know of white, we know of high because we know of low, we know of good because we know of evil. An extreme example of this would be studying our visual perception of the world if we lived in a completely white, or black, existence. In this world all things, ourselves included, would be the same color. For our example let's assume everything is pure white. Without contrast all would be equal. Without a visual comparison there would be no difference. We couldn't even consider the color black because we would have nothing to compare it to. If that scenario would hold for the spiritual realm we could know that all was equal. In either case, though, how could we call it "good" or any other thing? Good is only good because of its contrast with bad.

Our world is not monochromatic; we do have contrast. We know good from bad and we can make the comparison. Because we can make the comparison both must exist. Granted, we have degrees of such things and we can, at least on a social level, argue the complications of the shades of contrast. What I believe is acceptable you might categorize as wrong. Such things must be defined by our social context, the proper evaluation of our rule books, and, spiritually, by the basic original foundational premise. Consider this. If good and evil do exist, and an understanding of contrast shows they do, then we have reason to believe in their perfected form: Pure Good and Pure Evil.

In this quest, then, we are looking to engage one and hoping to avoid the other. We determine to choose our own path but if we don't know the options we have to ask, "What path am I on?"

This leads me to think of what I admire most from an opponent or competitor: subtlety, deception and camouflage. If I were the Director of Evil I wouldn't present myself with menace screaming in the school yard "Come here so I can torture you and cut you into little bits!" I'd politely, with a gentle smile upon my face say, "Hey little girl, would you like some candy?" I would consider my goal achieved if you believed that my true essence wasn't really there. If I was "black" and you were looking for "white" I'd achieve my goal by leading you to believe that "black" didn't exist. If black doesn't exist, then anything that you accept as true must be white. (See chapter 9).

So how do we know when something is actually good or if it is something bad in disguise? The only way I know is to study and understand the Truth so well that when you see something contrary it is boldly apparent. For instance, I think of the programs used in the U.S. and Britain to teach its officers about counterfeit currency. The class can be 40 hours long and during that time the officers only look at real, legal money. Never once do they study the plethora of counterfeit cash. They become so familiar with the real thing that when, finally someone puts a bad bill in their hands it immediately stands out. Something that you or I would not even notice is immediately apparent to these trained officers.

This assignment is harder in a spiritual quest because the line is blurred between what is good and what is deceit. For instance, where does the writer of this message lie on that continuum? How do you find the truth to study to be able to recognize readily the counterfeit? That is a touchy subject. I have my answer after spending years exploring the options that I wanted to be true and finally proving to myself what really made sense according to logic and science. (That is a presentation I will make later.) This requires that we take a stand on self denial and be willing to subject ourselves to the scientific process, even if it opposes our desired truth.

It might be said that science proves that there is no such thing as God so if we use those rules God disappears. Keep this in mind. Science once believed that our universe was eternal, always here always will be. Then Einstein came along with that relativity thing and showed that there had to be a beginning and the 2nd law of thermodynamics proved that this universe is breaking down so it won't be here forever. As I write this down the scientific community is beginning to embrace the belief that there is no way we could have come to be without the involvement of and intelligent designer. If this keeps up science will easily prove the existence of God. A God who, by the way, created the natural laws we use to try to prove he doesn't exist. Also note that many of the early scientists, who brought us theories still in use today, were also theists.

I urge you to seek the Truth, to understand why it makes sense, to never allow yourself to believe that your faith must be blind and to know that your system should be expected to stand up to the hard questions. Study until you know it so well that the deception won't likely occur to you. This requires the characteristics listed in chapter 3, Playing by the rules.

I watched a movie recently called "End of Days" with Arnold Schwartzenagger as the protagonist. The premise was that at the last hour of the millennium, 1999, the Devil was to physically engage a human to produce a child who would become the Anti-Christ. Having done some study into comparative religions

I noted some inconsistency in what I knew of the Christian point of view. For instance the sign of the beast represented in the book of Revelations and in an older movie, "The Omen", as 666 was different here. The movie stated that because in dreams we sometimes see things backwards or upside-down, the real mark of the beast is 999- as in 1999 when the movie takes place. (Why not the year 999 or 2999?) More anomalies presented themselves and they made me wonder who would check them out after watching the film? Who would walk away believing the information presented here then pass it on to others as "fact"? If taken as fact it would either cause people to live in fear of this possibility or cause people to write off the Christian point of view as laughable. Any worldview should be judged by its merits *and not its abuses*. If either point of view of the above is to be held it should be held from the position of true knowledge not feeling, speculation and sensationalism.

Of greater concern is when people who profess that they are of a particular spiritual worldview speak of their rulebook with misunderstanding or misinterpretation but do so with authority. In Islam, for instance, there are those who profess it to be a religion of peace. There are others who use it as their reason to kill non-believers in the name of Allah. They both speak with authority but who double checks them? The potential for blind followers is there but is ultimately the responsibility of the follower. They must double check the information given to them. Someone can lead me to believe in a false doctrine because of their authority, but I need to carefully check to be sure that they are not presenting misinformation.

The other outcome is to push away potential believers because of being caught in an inconsistency. This, of course, only matters ultimately if that person is actually following a truthful doctrine.

I did some training at a wilderness school in the eastern U.S. which is run by a man who has written numerous books and is renown in his field. I was excited to be able to finally meet the man who wrote the books which had become very important to me. I also wanted to sit in his class and learn from this authority figure. He repeated this line in many of his classes, "your job is to prove me right or prove me wrong and I bet you can't prove me wrong". I was very impressed. How could one not trust the authority of someone who was so respected and who was so confident to be able to pose such a challenge? Ultimately I didn't try very hard. I felt since I was able to prove the obvious things to be true I probably could trust the rest. So I trusted the rest.

One day I found a flaw in one of his spiritual teachings; a slight error and a reason to finally take him up on his challenge. When I did the research I found several inconsistencies and much more reason to believe that much of who he professed to be may be a fabrication. Some of what he taught was solid but I found myself double-checking and experimenting with everything. My mind went back to the Monopoly incident and solidified the fact that I needed to probe a bit more. I still use his books and teach techniques that I first learned from him but now

I take everything as potentially wrong until further research confirms, or denies, his facts. I then only use the things that I can prove in what I teach.

There is a process that needs to be used to determine the truth. If we take in new information, do some follow up research then make a determination we have begun well. Sometimes I find I lock into information as truth only to find more information later that debunks the truth I had known. I then continue the process until I can really rely on it.

When it comes to spiritual truth there are so many options but the main criteria has to be that the essential rules of the rulebook always have to be followed and the rulebook itself has to have internal consistency and fundamental trustworthiness. So, any worthy belief system has essentials that need to be adhered to by everyone who professes to follow that system, even if there are peripheral issues that can be debated. For example, in the Christian doctrine an essential is that one must believe that Jesus of Nazareth was God in human flesh, He came to earth to die for the sins of humanity and his resurrection was a sign of the resurrection of believers in Christ into heaven. A peripheral issue is whether or not the world was created in 6 literal days. If you adhere to the first doctrine, according to the Christian faith, your salvation is assured even if you debate a six day or a six era creation scenario.

The trouble with some presentations is when leaders and teachers use partial truths and out of context interpretation to lead people astray. This is often done so the teacher will benefit, but at the expense of the student. Keep in mind that this can happen unintentionally by someone who truly believes what they teach but as of yet hasn't done all of the investigation needed in their situation. An example of that would be that in the Christian faith you only have to believe that Jesus of Nazareth was a prophet or an exceptional teacher. If you take the Godhood out of that equation it changes the essential doctrine according to conservative Christians.

I know a woman who does Angelic Healing and learning of her practice lead me to this sort of investigation. I was the Program Director for an exclusive spa and she wanted to do her work for our guests. When I first got her letter I discarded the idea. It didn't seem like a program that made sense and I did no research. Later she contacted me again and during that conversation she told me my deceased grandfather wanted to pass on a message to me. She related the message and I listened politely. She also sent me a letter with the information from my grandfather recorded on it.

It said:

"Randy, my boy, you have walked a long path. A path of learning. You have learned much on this path of yours and now is the time to let the past be the past. To take this learning and bring it to the present. To use it to assist others, to teach others of what you have learned.

"It is time for you to remember the master that you are, the Master of life. It is time to heal the pain that is within you and walk proud in who you are, who you have become. You have finished your lessons in life and now is the time to teach, to teach what you know, what you have learned to those who will listen, those who can benefit from your learning.

"I, we (all who have come before you) are proud of you and all that you have accomplished. Remember that you are never alone, there are many beings standing with you and assisting you.

Keep your chin up and always look forward."

This is how it was sent to me verbatim. The first thing I noticed was that the greeting was unlike how my grandfather talked to me and there was a particular line he would have used in the end of the message that was missing. The second thing is nothing specific is cited that ties the message to me and if you change the name, and gender if necessary, this is a message that could pertain to any number of people. Apply it to yourself. Do my "grandfathers" words even remotely ring true to you? It appears to me that for someone who feels a little low and needs some encouragement that their life was going OK, these were words that they could hang their hat on. This is a very generic piece of information that could be bent by most folks to receive encouragement.

It didn't sit right with me though. Ever the skeptic I called and asked a few questions. It was during that call that she told me that Jesus Christ had come to her and started guiding her to heal people. He also introduced her to a Main Hindu deity because if she knew him/her she could help to heal people of other belief systems.

My research into Christian belief indicated that there was some inconsistency either in her information or in what Christians held to be the essentials of their beliefs. The Christian rulebook gives a harsh warning that speaking to the spirits of the dead was an abomination to God (Deuteronomy 18:10-12) and that Christ claimed to be the only way for men to reach God (John 14:6). So no matter what you or I believe this entity that spoke through the Angel Lady could not be Christ because he contradicted himself. If he is the only way then he would not introduce people to other deities because the Bible states that all others are false gods.

Warning alarms came up at this point. Either she was lying, whoever she was communicating with was lying or the Christian rulebook was lying.

I did my research and I believe she was sincere. The rest I leave to you at this point. No matter what I say I found you will still have to double check my work. If the contrast of the two remaining options strikes you as incongruent then take a look around and see what you find.

Though it can be broken down even further, there are two definite types of outcomes to any discussion of religion or spiritual belief. We either react or respond. A response is a thought out reasoned way of handling a situation. A reaction is an emotional answer to a situation.

If we use the Ford versus Chevy analogy and I say Ford is best a fan of Chevy would respond by giving reasons why Chevy is better, tell me the reasons why Ford is inferior and tell me that I can like Ford products if I wish but I will be wrong.

A reaction would go something like this. Ford!?! The best!?! You have got to be kidding!?! Everyone knows that only fools and idiots would drive a Ford voluntarily. Chevy's have the best this and the best that and intelligent people all agree that to choose any other option is ludicrous!!!"

We must be careful not to confuse an emotional reaction with a passionate response. They can look similar but a reasoned dissection can separate one from the other. One can also give a reasonable response and still be wrong if the information used is somehow incomplete.

An obvious reason for a passionate response would be when harm might come to someone if the argument for the response isn't heeded. If an adult child of mine wanted to walk toward a cliff blindfolded to see if they could sense the edge before they walked off (because they had read a book on how to do such a thing) my reaction might be, "You have got to be kidding! Only a fool would attempt that voluntarily!!" But my response would be, "If that book has merit you may want to try your experiment first on things that won't cause you permanent harm, like sudden de-acceleration death syndrome. If you must practice this thing, try it out by drawing a line in the back yard and see if you can sense it blind-folded. Practice the technique to see if it works with a safety net before you trust this author on a discipline unexplored by you. When you can prove that the technique works every time, then you might want to move on."

"But", my child replies, "The author said what the subconscious mind senses is danger".

"Try this then" I'd respond. "Set a line of mouse traps in the yard and do the experiment barefooted." (The reaction would be, "Danger!?! You want danger!?! Why can't your subconscious sense what I'm about to do to you, you knot-head child!?)

Within both types of exchange you will feel emotion. The difference is that with the passionate response you can define the why of the emotion with the content of the argument. With response the emotion attached has to be rationalized because the argument, as stated, doesn't show the logical why of the emotion.

The adult child in this scene may give a response that seems to be rational to them with the information they have in their head. Two people can look at the same circumstance and interpret it differently based on their worldviews. This adds to the discussion the elements of subjectivity and objectivity. My dictionary defines the objectivity as "dealing with external facts and not with thoughts and feelings" and subjectivity as "introspection pertaining to the thinking subject." The first is the way to seek the truth even though it is improbable that we can do that without some personal feeling coming into the mix. We will always have presupposition. We are thinking objectively when we recognize that within our search.

Do right and wrong exist? Based on the earlier explorations in this chapter we can say they certainly do. The far ends of the spectrum of these two are definable and noticeable by nearly everyone. As we move to the center of the spectrum the contrast of the two gets easier to ignore. It becomes easier to rationalize something from the wrong side over to the right side with our subjectivity.

Now, if this understanding of right and wrong come to us from and entity greater than us we have a set of rules that objectively must be followed to stay on track with the side of right. We also have ways to rationalize subjectively that effectively argue that when we do something questionable it still should be considered on the side of right.

Remember the cartoons on television that show a character with a moral dilemma? There would always be an angel character on one shoulder trying to lead the person to do the right thing. On the other shoulder there was a devil character trying to push him to do *what he really wanted to do but* objectively knew to be wrong. This, as in all good comedy, worked for the audience because it stems from the truth.

The main character would look back and forth between the two and then make his choice. In the cartoons that come back to me now I can't recall a time when the main character took the high road. It seems we were always rooting for the devil guy to win. There is a natural temptation to strike out against the internal voice that knows the truth, when what we desire is not ethical or moral. Objectivity tells us one thing and subjectivity tells us another.

The next time you see one of these cartoons take note that the angel is usually responding and the devil is reacting by the end of the argument. They both start off calm and reasonable trying to nudge the character to go their way. Toward the end of the discussion if the devil side is losing usually he resorts to emotional reaction. Even in the cartoon world reaction becomes the strong suit to allow us to rationalize and accept the side we know internally to be wrong.

The contrast between right and wrong is already within us. One hint of that is the reaction I feel as I write and as you might feel as you read this. Is there a bit of "who does this guy think he is?" building? Right now, on my left shoulder I have a devil author saying, "Who do you think you are? You can't tell these people what to do. You can't even do it right yourself! "On my right shoulder the angel author is saying, "Keep writing, and let the people decide for themselves." The fact that I have a little devil sitting on my left shoulder telling me I have no right to talk to you this way gives me the indication that I should keep plugging away.

The little devil guy is gone now. Hey, what's that on your left shoulder?

5.

FAITH MUST FOLLOW LOGIC AND REASON

Faith is defined by my Webster's Dictionary as, "Complete acceptance of a truth which cannot be proved by process of logical thought." Faith by itself may not seem logical but it must have a foundation on which you can rely. That foundation must be built on logic. If it is not, emotion, which can be very persuasive in this debate, will have a definitive influence and your belief system can be discarded by others as based on feelings and speculation. If the foundation is built on a premise of logical thought, then the areas that do require real faith are easier to reconcile.

Think of someone who you trust implicitly, someone who when they speak you always tend to believe. When they joke with you, you always see the smile in their eyes and when they are serious that look prevails. If that person walked into your house, had that look of seriousness on their face and said, "The sky just turned purple." what would your response be as you followed them back outside? If your foundation was strong, based on years of trust and understanding, no matter what the logical mind was suggesting, you would be thinking, "How could this be?" and not "There is no way."

Logic would dictate that you check for yourself but your faith would lead you to believe your friend. You have no reason to have that sort of faith in me but I have seen a sky that can only be defined as purple during a Midwest thunder storm. With that explanation your logical brain probably can wrap around the idea where it's not tough to picture a purple sky. But whether told by a trusted friend or by someone unknown, like me, you most likely want to check it out for yourself. Faith is built up by information on a topic, or by a source, being continually proven true.

Another definition of faith is, "The substance of things hoped for, the evidence of things not seen." (Hebrews 11:1) How do we build our faith in the things of the spirit, those concepts that can't, by definition, be directly observed? If we can't see them, how do we have faith in them? How do we even have this conversation about the possibility of an unseen God? Something has to point to the possibility that the spiritual realm exists. We also have to have enough evidence in our physical world that builds a foundation for us to logically extend to the belief in something beyond it.

When I was a kid I lived in a haunted house. We had a gravestone in the back yard that told us who the ghost was but more importantly I heard her walking at night. I would wake up and hear footsteps coming down the hall to my room. I would be frightened beyond belief but fortunately she always stayed in the hall and never hurt me. When I got a bit older I got up when I heard the foot steps to be sure it wasn't just my sister messing with me. I'd wait until I thought she was close to the end of the hall then I would turn on my light. I never saw anything in the hall so I figured that the ghost just slipped through the wall when I turned on the light. It took me a few more years to consider that if she could go through walls how could she have enough weight to make the floor creak. I decided that there were no ghosts in my house on the day I sat in the well lit hall and listened to the floor creak when only I was there.

So when we talk of the things of the spirit we have to apply faith but how do we build a reasonable foundation? I found I have built up my faith in something just by wanting it to be so. During my quest, when a certain outcome was desired, I was able to convince myself of "logical" ways to achieve that outcome even without any evidence to back up my thoughts. The danger here was that I only had to convince myself. And I trusted myself. I ran into trouble when I had to explain my belief to others who were more critical. When I was forced to explain my belief logically I was forced to see the areas of illogic. There may be people who you can never convince even when your foundation is strong, but you should be able to reach an open minded person with the prospect that at least what you propose has a possibility. Your foundation has to have merit and be plausible. As I write I have picked up the pleasant scent of creosote bushes from my backyard. If you don't live in the desert and are familiar with the word creosote you probably think of the foul smelling product used to coat railroad ties and the buried parts of a fence posts to keep them from rotting. If this was your foundation and I told you that when it rains the creosote bush lets off the most wonderful fragrance and the whole desert smells good you'd think I was nuts or that I loved to sniff tar. If your only experience with the word creosote was the smell of railroad ties you'd not likely understand why I was so enthralled with the smell. If you came to the desert to visit me during the non-rainy season and I told you this, I would have to produce some evidence. So when I asked you to pinch some of the tiny leaves of the creosote plant, which we identified in the guidebook so that you would know I wasn't trying to substitute a different plant, you would probably do it and expect a petroleum smell. When you caught the scent of the actual plant oils your mind would be changed. Then when I said that the rain releases the scent throughout the whole area you'd have enough evidence to believe even though you have never been to the desert during the rainy season. So how do you know what you have faith in is true? There must be enough evidence for the things that are provable about your belief to be able to say "If this, this and that are provable then I know I can trust the other."

In the creosote example we proved enough evidence of the good smell of the plant oils and the ability of the scent to be released that you could go home to the Midwest and tell people how good the desert can smell after a rain even though you haven't been there during a rain yet. I took the time to verify my claim and I gave you enough evidence to give you faith in this set of facts that you have the confidence to pass it on without fear that you will be proven wrong by a skeptic.

I personally don't believe in evolution. When I was in school I did based on the evidence presented to me by my teachers. I had confidence in those men and women because they had spent years learning about and teaching these things. Because of my trust I was comfortable reciting what they taught me at the front of the classroom. Later, when I started looking deeper into the evidence I noticed inconsistencies and unreasonable logic. A big one was that a drawing in my school books of Nebraska Man who had been deduced from the discovery of one tooth. The books show 2 whole humans, one male and one female, conceived by the discovery of this one tooth.

It was later proven the tooth was from a pig. It appeared that the scientists so wanted evolution to be true that they were seeing their preconceived notions and not fully exploring other options. I started to have doubts about the users of the scientific method as it applied to this debate. One scientist, Coppedge, stated that the probability of a single protein molecule being arranged by chance is 1 in 10 to the 161st power. And it takes 239 of these proteins to make up the simplest life forms. This may seem plausible to the casual observer but Borel's Law changes that. Emil Borel, a mathematical scientist, stated that any probability beyond 10 to the 50th power is so remote that it can virtually never occur. (1 chance in 10 to the 12th power is one in a trillion) winning a standard lottery with 6 numbers is 1 in 21 million. How often does your ticket hit all six numbers?

The evidence of irreducible complexity (as described by Michael Behe in "Darwin's Black Box") also suggests that there are mechanisms within all living systems that have multiple parts and all of the parts need to be present in order for the system to function. Also, each of these parts by themselves serves no valuable purpose. Remove one piece and the whole thing falls apart. This occurs even in the "simple cell" so often taught about in my classes on evolution. Even Darwin stated "If it could be demonstrated that any complex organ existed which could not possibly have been formed by numerous, successive, slight modifications, my theory would absolutely break down." (Origin of Species 6th edition New York University Press).

Science has discovered numerous systems that match that description in all life forms from simple to complex. So what seemed logical to me at one point has proven to be illogical with further study. My initial faith in those high school teachers was unfounded. My faith, at the time, was complete but it wasn't based on verifiable evidence, it was based on my trust in the authority of my teachers. When I started doing deeper research I found many holes in the theory of evolution and much mathematical and logical evidence that showed the improbability of us coming about in that step by step manner. To those that I have offended with this revelation let me say that I am still open to debate and will consider any logical and reasoned source of information to sway me back. So far I haven't found any.

The scientific method is designed not to just find evidence to prove a theory right but to see if the theory can be proven wrong. In proper research both sides are being presented. The basics of the scientific method include:

Asking a question, forming a hypothesis based on that question, developing an experimental procedure to test the hypothesis, keeping records of the results and forming a conclusion based on those results.

We must be able to do the same with the quest for spiritual truth. In the physical world a theory is often put forth with faith in a particular outcome. The evidence then comes in to either prove or disprove the premise. The scientist starts with faith and looks to provide the evidence. He challenges others to try to change his point of view and if he is doing the job in the true scientific way he wants the final outcome to be solidly provable. Even if it goes against his original theory. We have many examples of such things going on in our world of science. Think of what you have heard about nutrition over the years. Fat is bad for you vs. low fat diets have made us an obese nation. Carbohydrates should be the staple of a healthy diet vs. eat more meat and cut the carbohydrates to lose weight. And so on. You can always find evidence and statistics to prove your point of view. If you don't allow all the evidence to enter the debate you are only trying to prove your truth, not The Truth.

The quest for spiritual truth has an element that makes direct contact and physical proof impossible. You can't see a spirit. If we can be so far apart in our scientific theories in the physical world you can imagine why we have so many religious theories to choose from. Faith then becomes a vital element. We may be able to find enough evidence to satisfy some people while others looking at the same evidence will shake their heads and walk away perplexed at how anyone could be so naive or narrow-minded or so easily duped.

So in this quest your foundation has to be solid enough to support a reasonable faith. And reasonable faith has to be considered fair even if we can't show the same evidence as we can with the equation of 2+2=4. (No faith is involved there once you know the mathematical rules.)

What evidence do we need to safely say that we believe certainly and assuredly in a God that we can't see or show directly to others? Conversely, what evidence do we need to convince others to believe in a universe that has no God when the evidence leans toward intelligent design? Something of our theory needs to have solid evidential proof. We must be able to logically prove our point through reason, historical evidence and science. Some of the evidence may be circumstantial but circumstantial evidence has been used numerous times to convict a guilty person of a crime. When we do this our evidence has to be presented in a form that is universally accepted.

In trying to prove to a disbeliever I can't prove that a ghost existed in my childhood home with just the evidence that at night I heard footsteps and my sister heard them too so with corroborating evidence you must believe. My belief in something that can just as easily be dismissed by other evidence cannot be the historic evidence I rely upon to prove my point. The ghost stories of my youth are true. My sister and I still talk about them over lunch on occasion. The question is was it just the fearful wandering minds of two children or did a ghost wander the halls of our home? When I tell the stories of our ghost many believe that it was really a ghost even though I have enough evidence now to have changed my mind on the subject. The fact that I can find many around the world who believe in ghosts is not enough evidence. I still need to supply solid evidence that shows that ghosts could exist even if some won't be convinced. Keep in mind that there are those who still doubt that we put a man on the moon or that the Holocaust occurred.

Ultimately you are responsible for what you believe. You must be confident in your belief and you should be able to give reasonable answers as to why you have this confidence. You should have historic, scientific and mathematical evidence to back up your reasonable claims and you should be able to counter my reasonable doubts with the same evidence. This debate has to occur on the response level not the reaction level. (Emotion is always allowed though). My reasonable doubts need to be countered with reasonable evidence.

We need to avoid taking the route of blind faith. My faith comes from years of searching and finding during that search the foundation of my beliefs. How can we know that the foundation upon which we rely is solid?

We believe that the sun will rise tomorrow morning. What evidence do we have that this will happen? The most obvious is prior daily repetition. But what if we arrived here at noon today from another world? On our world the sun was constant and provided the heat and light we needed from a fixed point. As the day progressed and we noticed the sun movement we would be concerned. At sunset, as the heat and light faded, we would panic thinking it was the end of the world. Our hosts would tell us not to worry because this happens everyday. Tomorrow the sun will rise again and the process will repeat.

We are not convinced. We notice that our hosts seem calm and they claim to have seen it before but *we've* never seen it. Besides, how can we trust these people we don't even know?

"There is proof", they say and they lead us to the local library. They point us to the stacks of books on celestial science. It may be written and scientific to their minds but to us it is still theory because we haven't experienced the proof. Because of our fear we decide to do some reading and we begin to see the logic of the mechanisms of the solar system. We see how the early astronomers, before modern technology, had differing views on what was the center of this solar system and how the changes in thought came about with time and technology. We might still have doubts. Maybe this stuff was written just to appease people like us. We decide that with what we have read, coupled with the evidence that no one appears to be panicked, we will have some faith.

We are fast and voracious readers and we eagerly consume volumes of scientific and mythological text. With both sides of the story presented we can see where science prevails and how the myths could evolve from such natural happenings, i.e. eclipses, etc.

Four hours before the alleged sunrise we have gone through enough study to convince us that, even without trusting the past history of these believers, the scientific information holds true. Now we can comfortably, and with solid faith, drift off to sleep knowing not only that the sun will rise but knowing when with scientific clarity.

This scenario is the proper way to approach faith in our quest. Certainly some will be drawn by the words of a trusted friend and that will be enough. But for most some proof is needed. When I first looked into belief in a specific God I said, "I'll have faith when you give me proof." I was told that it didn't work that way, and my logical brain confirmed it. Faith is confident belief without physical proof. Proof is evidence establishing the truth of something. They seem to be opposite concepts. So how can a person prone to logical thought have a confirmed faith? They can do it with evolution of thought. Once we get our presuppositions out of the way, we will find that there are those faiths that don't require unproven belief. In fact proof abounds!

We use science, logic and historical reliability even when some say God and reason don't mix. Archeology is a defined, reliable science and its use should be able to corroborate the claims of all historic religious beliefs. Archeological evidence should be able to verify the claims laid out by the founders of a faith and the historic claims they put forth. In this quest can history prove that the people existed and that what was claimed by them and about them actually did happen?

There are many people important to religious traditions whose existence can be proven by history. I don't think there is any real controversy that Moses, Mohammed, Jesus, Gautama (the Buddha) or Joseph Smith were figures in history. There are also the artifacts of other faiths that are here to be seen and felt like the original sacred pipe said to have been given to the Lakota people by the Buffalo Calf Woman. The question becomes can we weave the historical accounts of the people with the proof of the artifacts that fit with their story and have enough evidence, based on science, to substantiate their claims? Keep in mind that there is still room for faith but that faith must have a solid foundation.

I can touch the sacred pipe of the Lakota but can I prove the story of how it came to be? I can read the words of Mohammed but can I prove to your satisfaction that he presented them, by himself, inspired by the Angel of God? I can find solid proof that the Buddha lived but do I have substantial proof that he reached enlightenment? I can find the proof of Jesus' life in history but can I prove that he rose from the dead?

That is the meat of this quest. We must prove objectively that the whole thread runs through the fabric of our belief and be able to make a logical case that will hold up to the fair scrutiny of people who don't understand your faith.

I think of Santa and the Easter Bunny. How does one prove they exist to an adult who is influenced by the research of his childhood? I don't want to give anything away here but consider what the point is, where it comes from and when your discovery of the truth occurred. Who believes what and when do they alter their belief?

Coins under the pillow and gifts under the tree are evidence enough for the youngest but when suspicion starts other things are needed to keep the faith alive. My kids saw the teeth marks in the carrots left for the Bunny and the half consumed milk and cookies left for Santa as evidence that those characters were there as they got older. We know how these stories turn out but how do we flesh out our stories of faith to be certain that they are true? How do we avoid being in the position of our children who ultimately go through a bit of trauma in their enlightenment?

We start out with the idea that we need to build a solid foundation for our faith with a preponderance of evidence for those things that we can have evidence to prove and a faith built on that foundation. We often have faith first, and that's OK as long as we do the work to build the foundation underneath without too much presupposition.

There is nothing wrong with expecting a logical background for your faith. It is too easy to be swayed in the direction of a myth or fairy tale if we don't.

6.

CIRCUMSTANTIAL EVIDENCE

◆═◎═◆

Sherlock Holmes in "The Beryl Coronet" concluded "It's an old maxim of mine that when you have excluded the impossible, whatever remains, however improbable, must be the truth". The question "If there is a God, and if there is life after death, then why can't these things be proved?" was asked by the Christian philosopher Thomas V. Morris in his book "Making Sense of it All." The nineteenth century mathematician W. K. Clifford stated "It is always wrong, for anyone anywhere to believe anything without sufficient evidence."

There does not seem to be any solid, physical evidence of the existence of a God. We can point to things that we surmise are from God then assume his existence but you can't point to God, as you can to me, and say "there he is. Pinch him, he is right there".

So how do we know for sure without going into the nebulous, "I just feel is must be so" attitude, and show some of the evidence that Clifford demands? With circumstantial evidence.

Circumstantial evidence is defined by Webster's as: "based on incidental (casual, minor) details". One has to be careful when weighing circumstantial evidence. But if it can be used to convict someone of a crime, we should be able to include it with other details to make a case for the existence of a God we cannot see directly.

How does circumstantial evidence fit in? As a park ranger the best way for me to make an arrest stick was to have caught the bad guy in the act of breaking the law. If I saw a picnicker throw a soda can and then walk away, I had definitive evidence to write a ticket for littering. If I saw a piece of litter next to a picnic table occupied by picnickers that wouldn't be enough evidence to arrest anyone at the table for littering; even if the litter on the ground was the same as the products on the table.

Let's say that I walk through the picnic area and see 3 guys sitting at a table, and all three are have soft drinks in front of them. One is drinking Coke, one is drinking Pepsi and one is drinking R.C. Cola. The only cans in front of each individual are their brand of choice. All three picnickers have empty cans within their reach but the only cans on the ground are the R. C. Cola cans. The R.C. cans on the ground are near the side of the table of the R.C. drinker and all three people are laughing and talking and uncon-cerned about the litter. I haven't seen anyone toss a can but the circumstantial evidence points to the R.C. guy as the one who tossed the litter.

We have other possible options though. It could have been the Pepsi guy who tossed his pals cans to get him in trouble. The Pepsi guy looks shady but there is other evidence that brings us back to the R.C. guy. If the Pepsi guy had done that the R.C. guy would be upset and trying to get the Pepsi guy to clean up the mess. If that didn't work he would be tossing Pepsi cans around for revenge. But as I approach no trouble is afoot and they all seem to be getting along just fine.

So in the final analysis we haven't seen the act but all the circumstantial evidence points to the R.C. guy.

1) He is the only one drinking R.C.
2) R.C. cans are the only ones on the ground.
3) The cans are all near him.
4) He doesn't seem to be concerned that his cans are on the ground.
5) We have the potential eyewitness evidence of his pals and other picnickers to corroborate our premise.

Even without the eyewitness accounts, though, we have a fairly tight case.

In our spiritual quest when do we have enough information to be able to say, beyond a reasonable doubt, that the God we believe in exists? Even though we are dealing in faith we must appeal to logic and reason. If I want a certain outcome I will focus on one piece of evidence that I can conform to my way of thinking. If I had decided that the guilty party was that lowly Pepsi guy he is where I would focus my attention. I'd rationalize that is was him because he looked shady and he was sitting right next to the R.C. guy so he must have knocked those cans over to make the R.C. guy look guilty. No matter how he proclaimed his innocence I'd downplay it, rationalize it away and cart him off to the hoosegow.

When it comes to the spiritual quest that sort of rationalization is common. We tend to want what we want and we avoid the obvious if it doesn't conform to the outcome we desire. The logic doesn't fit and the evidence for another explanation is obvious yet a desire for something to be true overshadows the logical evidence.

For some people there is an incongruity mixing science and religion. Therefore there is reluctance in agreeing that you can prove one with the other because they are on opposite ends of the spectrum. So how do we use science to prove the existence of a spiritual realm that is not yet measurable by our machinery? We could begin to approach the answer by building on the logical assumptions of peripheral evidence.

Leonardo da Vinci died almost 500 years ago. I never met him so as a human he is as real to me as any other human from 500 years ago. I've heard that he was an artist and an inventor. But how do I really know? I've heard that Bigfoot exists and that there are plaster casts of its foot prints, but I have seen as many da Vinci's as I have Bigfoot's. (Or is that Bigfeet?)

Historically then, how do I prove to myself, and more importantly to others, that da Vinci was real? One possibility would be through his art. As a non-believer in da Vinci-ism I could point out that this alleged art comes to us five centuries after the fact of his alleged existence. I would have to concede, though, that we have evidence that places da Vinci at a certain time and place in history and even people who don't embrace the art have verified that he was about during that time and place. There are those who say I don't know art but this da Vinci guy worked for the Duke of Milan as a military engineer and he designed fortresses and artillery. He was also a civil engineer and did the same kind of creation of locks for canals. We even find plans for a sculpture he was commissioned to do of the Duke's father. This would lead us to the possibility that he had something to do with art after all.

If we search the historical writings of the time we will be able to verify people who knew him and connected him with the art and that art can be traced back to a time and place where he could have created it. For us skeptics this is all circumstantial but it seems like enough to have to admit that this guy was around and he was an artist.

So now I can go to a gallery filled with his art and see the beauty and artistry of his hand and believe that man existed through the observation of his art. I can verify the man through his works.

On the other end of that kind of research is the existence of Bigfoot. Recently the family of Ray L. Wallace revealed that Mr. Wallace created the modern myth of Bigfoot by carving plywood "feet" to lay tracks around the construction sites where he worked. The family tells of how he orchestrated the filming of Bigfoot by telling the photographer where he might see the creature and then being sure the creature showed up. Wallace said he knew who was in the suit at the planned filming site.

There are those who still believe that a creature like Bigfoot does exist and that there is persuasive evidence of that fact. According to a December 6, 2002 article in the Arizona Daily Star "Jeff Meldrum, an associate professor of anatomy and anthropology at Idaho State University, says he has casts of 40 to 50 footprints he believes were made by authentic, unknown primates."

" 'To suggest all these are explained by carved feet strapped to boots just doesn't wash,' Meldrum said, noting 19th-century accounts of such a creature."

Still there are no bones, or hide or other physical evidence that has been found that can substantiate the claim. We have no physical evidence, other than the footprints which can be contested, of Bigfoot to place him in the same category of da Vinci.

How then do we give solid evidence when trying to prove the existence of God? The proof of His existence falls somewhere between the sort of proof we have for da Vinci and the sort of proof we have for Bigfoot. Can we see God? No, but we can see his work and his artistry. Scientifically as we look at nature and the cosmos we can see very specific signs of intelligent design. If you found a new car in your back yard you wouldn't assume that it just happened to be put together as a product of nature. You wouldn't say "Gee. This is cool. I haven't been back here for a while and look at the Ford that evolved. Maybe if I wait it will turn into a Mercedes." You would have to conclude that someone put it there. The same has to be true for the existence of the universe. The machinery of even the simplest cell is more complex than the Ford in your backyard so how can we assume the things of this world were accidental?

It was once thought that the universe was eternal, that time and chance could produce such complexity. Einstein gave us the science that points toward a specific point of origin for all that is around us in his Theory of Relativity. So if it began it had to begin from something and the law of cause and effect states that the cause has to be greater than the effect. This has science pointing toward a creator that is much more complex than the creation. I look at my computer as a perfect example. No matter how complex it appears it still can't do more than the human who designed the formulas that make it function. I am not a computer person and as I type out these words on my laptop I consider it a machine that I feel I have no right to own because of its complexity. I still have no idea what it can do and computer people tell me that I am only using a small fraction of what I could be doing with it. Still, the functions it can perform are primitive compared to what is happening with my eyes, brain, and motor function as I type these words into the computer. Even as I transpose already written words from the handwritten page to the screen my human machinery is performing functions every second far more complex than any this machine on my desk could ever do.

The theory of creation states that a being far more complex than us working outside of our normal time and space continuum placed us and all that is around us here. The Big Bang theory states that first there was nothing, then that nothing exploded to eventually evolve into what we have around us. Using Sherlock Holmes's quote from the beginning of this chapter which of these two has the best chance of being true? Since it is impossible for "nothing" to be present, and for it to explode, we have to look at the other option, no matter how improbable, as being true.

The circumstantial evidence that suggests a God, at least in part, is in the artistry of His creation. We can't see the Artist but the art work is evident everywhere. Another piece of circumstantial evidence is that historically, in all cultures of the earth, people have believed in a God. We may not be able to agree on the details but if all cultures had a belief in a God could they all be wrong or might there have been a common reason for this belief?

Something that was touched upon earlier was the fact that all cultures have common agreement on moral issues. If multiple cultures from all over the world share basic moral principals we could safely assume that those morals come from a common cause. That larger cause gives us the common effect. Culturally we have diluted the original intent but we can still point to a common starting point. I'm reminded of the telephone game. Early on God whispered into our ear and the continual process of us passing on the message, with the changes that make us comfortable, has degraded the message. This goes beyond mere coincidence.

In this part of the quest some questions need to be asked. The answers to these questions can move the evidence from circumstantial to something more solid. Look at the questions listed below from the point of view of your belief system. Look to your rule book to see how it answers each one. The answers should be there and have sufficient evidence so that they can be logically presented to others.

1) Where did we come from? (If we were designed, who designed us?)

2) Why are we here? (What was the purpose of our designer?)

3) Is our world perfect as it is? (Even if everything happens for a reason I think it is safe to say that our world has a way to go before it can be called perfect.)

4) What can we do to get our world to that state of perfection? (What does your rulebook say?)

The answers to these questions should be within everyone's worldview. With research we should be able to answer these questions to our satisfaction and to the satisfaction of the logical mind of a seeker.

Where did we come from? The scientific law of cause and effect states that the "Who", who put us here has to be smarter with higher moral standards and outside of our current constraints. If you believe we were put here by beings from another solar system, that's fine, but we need to answer this question without stopping at an intermediary. If all life seen and unseen was created, we need to get straight to the source. Who created those beings so they could create us? So look at your rule book. How is creation and the creator defined and do they have a logical explanation?

It is fair to say that a logical explanation has to be presented in steps. We tend to want one line answers even to complex issues, but for questions of this magnitude it takes time to build a foundation that is solid enough to hold them up. If someone were to ask you "Where did we come from?" And you answered "God, or Allah, or Vishnu, or The Infinite Universe", how does that satisfy the seeker of truth without first defining what is meant by your answer. I believe that it can be shown they are not different names for the same being. (See chapter 7.)

The seeker must first be willing to hear out what you mean by your one word or one phrase answer. If they want a quick, flip, one sentence answer, they most likely will be disappointed. If they accept a quick, flip, one sentence answer, you should be disappointed.

No matter what we believe spiritually we must believe it deeply and passionately. Any superficial belief needs to be deepened with, or discarded by, research, study and practice. We also should be able to follow the rules of science. Though it is not necessary for faith, try following the procedure used by scientist. Form a theory, put it to the test, prove it right or wrong and keep going. What deepens faith more than anything is not to blindly defend a passionate belief but to get out and see if you can find fault, to lovingly see if it can be disproved. That way, if somebody comes to you with a hard question you can reply with "That's a good point. I wondered about that myself." You can then give a reasoned answer from the research you have done. The other result will be that you won't be surprised by the hard questions. Let's face it. They will be with us as long as we ponder the things of the spirit. In this life we will never have all of the answers. My hope is that we do the work so that we have complete confidence in the answers we do have.

As we seek we are more likely to be swayed by a reasoned answer than one based on just feelings. If you posed a serious question that you struggled with such as "How can there can be a loving God when there is so much pain in the world?", which type of answer would you most likely consider? "That's a good question. I struggled with that and here's what my research lead me to…" or "The spirits touched me on that question and now I feel this way…"

Does that mean that feelings don't play a part? No, but remember the last time you bought a lottery ticket because you had a feeling and your numbers still didn't come up? Math is solid, feelings are transitory. All I am saying is that we need more than feelings to prove or disprove our faith. I am often overjoyed without knowing why, and there are times that I go through periods of being upset without knowing why. During these times my foundation still keeps me on track with my faith. Feelings may lead you to a truth but that truth still should be verified with research to make your foundation strong.

Logic and reason are built into our brain and therefore must be there for a reason. If our creator put them there they must be usable to determine if that creator truly exists, at least circumstantially. The trouble with our interpretation of the rules of science is that it is hard to quickly determine the possibility of a Being that exists outside of our space and time so we find ways to discount the possibility. Within the debate about God, science is best known for using the logic and reason within us to disprove the possibility that it was designed by a God.

So how do we tie it all together? How do we go from "there has to be something more than just me living to pay the bills" to a faith in a religious system based on more than "I just want it to be so?" (It has been argued that we invented God because we didn't want to face the fact that we lived for 70 years then the lights went out. Our desperation for more leads us to invent an afterlife).

Consider this: If logic and reason were put in our brain for a purpose maybe the desire to seek God was placed there as well. Here is where the work starts. Here is where we can put into play the first few chapters and really dig in. For some people being convinced comes easy, others search for a long time. I won't pretend that there is an easy answer. My quest was a lifetime of passive searching coupled with 9 years of really pondering and working things through. The one thing that I believe, though, is that if you truly want to understand the truth and are open to the possibility of changing your worldview, the truth will be presented to you. Can I prove that? Not quickly but it fits upon my foundation.

Even if all of your evidence at this stage is circumstantial, it is time to build and solidify your foundation.

7.

CAN THERE BE MORE THAN ONE TRUTH?

There are numerous topics where you can compile a list of truths and all of them are accurate but that list still doesn't reveal the whole truth. Let's say you and I each are holding a candy bar, and a researcher is trying to determine if we each have the same brand of candy bar hidden in our hand.

The questions he might ask and the corresponding answers could include:

"Does it contain chocolate?"
We both would answer "Yes".
"Do they have peanuts?"
Again we both answer, "Yes".
"How about caramel?"
"Yes".
"Are they chewy?"
"Yes".

"If they both contain chocolate is that chocolate on the outside of the candy bar?"

"Yes".

The researcher decides at this point that he has enough information and he concludes:

"You both have the same brand of candy bar".

To verify his conclusion we open our hands and in mine there is a Snickers® and in yours is a Baby Ruth®. Up to this point all of our answers have been true so there is more than one truth. Where the researcher went wrong was that he didn't follow through. He found similarities and made an early conclusion. In this case there were many truths but if he continued searching he would have revealed an ultimate truth. We both had candy bars and though similar they have differences that are irreconcilable. (Yet another that fits, so far, is a chocolate covered Payday®.)

When it comes to our quest we have a similar problem. On the surface many belief systems have similarities but does that make them completely compatible? If I say there is a God and you proclaim the truth of Atheism we are diametrically opposed. Both concepts can't be right. Even if we can agree on some of life's principals one of us is ultimately wrong. Either there is a God or there isn't. There can be no middle ground.

If there is such a thing as truth then there must be such a thing as ultimate truth. In some things it may not matter. In the example of the candy we can choose. If all we want is the enjoyment of the sugar rush either will do. In the quest for spiritual truth if there is an ultimate truth, then we have a reason to believe knowing that truth will make an ultimate difference.

An honest look at religious belief will reveal that we can place most of them in the same category superficially. Just like our candy bar example they may have similar characteristics and even some of the internal ingredients will correspond. If you probe the essential doctrines of each, those things that are absolutely required to be a true devotee, you will see those irreconcilable differences appear.

We have three choices in the world religions: Monotheism, Polytheism, and Atheism; One God, Many Gods, or no God. If the choices were defended over a cup of coffee by a Jew, a Hindu and a Buddhist how would the story be reconciled? The Buddhist would say that there is no God so both of you are wrong. The Jew would say that there is a God but only one, so both of you are wrong. The Hindu would say there are many gods that exist so one of you is wrong and the other just hasn't met the other gods and so has clumped them all together as one. The Atheist would agree with the Jew; two of you are wrong, but would disagree on the reason; because there is no God.

With all of the possibilities of all the possible belief systems and all of them contrary to one another, even within our three categories, we still have a dilemma.

For direction I turn to Blaise Pascal, a 17th century mathematician who put forth a premise now known as "Pascal's Wager". In the wager he gives a way to determine the potential reward to the potential risk as it pertains to his belief in only one God, and a specific one in his mind, to the other options. He starts with a presupposition and uses logic and math to defend it.

The basic premise of Pascal's Wager is that if he believes in X and you believe in Y there are three possible outcomes.

1) He is right and you are wrong.
2) You are right and he is wrong.
3) You both are wrong.

The question, placed in the form of the logic of the bet, is what is the risk of loss versus the gain of reward? His belief was that belief in God would result in a life after death that was joyous and infinite. If the opposing view was that there is no God, and what you find after death is darkness, Pascal believed that the risk of betting your current life for the possibility of an eternal, carefree life was well worth it.

The wager then is this. In order to win the possibility of eternal happiness I have to wager the life I live now. There are rules I will have to live by based on the rulebook of this faith which may be hard to adjust to but in the end the ultimate reward is eternal happiness. The opposing bet is that I can do as I please in this life but risk the shot at an eternal happiness. Boiled down, the wager results in a bet of one life to win an infinite prize. And the odds, based on the above formula, are 33%. If you were told that you had a 1 in 3 chance to win a lottery, the bet was one dollar and the reward was an infinite amount of money would you take the bet? Pascal said that with the mathematical odds you'd be foolish not to.

Another way to look at this is what are the consequences for our non-belief?

When we look at all of the possibilities it can be overwhelming. We have to consider all of the options with a deep awareness. On my desk In front of me I have the descriptions of dozens of religions all of which have similarities and all of which have irreconcilable differences. To name a few we have, Judaism, Christianity, Hinduism, Buddhism, Islam, Confucianism, Taoism, a plethora of nature based faiths and so on. In the beginning of a spiritual quest how does one choose the program that they want to adhere to? They all have their premises and doctrines but to use the flip side of Pascal's Wager how about if we look at the consequences of unbelief instead of the reward of belief. It doesn't matter if you believe in the religion whose consequence you choose; just find the worst case scenario for unbelief.

In the above list Christianity has to be a contender with its doctrine of eternal separation from God and the unavoidable torment experienced as a result. Here is how I proceed. I need to be passionate enough about what I believe, and why I believe it, to be willing to suffer the worst possible consequence if I am wrong. That is easy to say but in order to make this a viable exercise we have to believe that the consequence is possible. If we do, then the logic we use to describe our faith has to be solid and our passion has to be strong.

How's your passion? Life should be lived with passion and your spiritual life should be lived with the ultimate passion. If you are not passionate about your spiritual stand there may be something more to explore. Our spiritual life has to be affected by our physical life. Thinking about what we do today may have little consequence; eat breakfast, empty the trash, go to Home Depot to buy some paint. It may be a bit more important; eat breakfast, finish the O'Malley proposal, close the 2 million dollar deal and make partner in the company. Or it may be bigger still; eat breakfast, walk to work, get hit by a bus and enter into eternity.

As we think about spiritual truth we have to ponder what that means. Do the lights just go out? Do we enter into another reality? Do we get sent back to this reality again with the intent to do better? Do we go to live in Heaven? Do we enter into the lake of fire? How do we know for sure and what is it that we want to be the truth? It is easy to say one or another outcome can't be true. But if the reason we give is it is not true because "I wouldn't do that if I were God" we need to go back to logic and reason to make our choice.

Keep in mind that the truth is the truth no matter what we believe. If the possible consequence of my wager is dire I want to be sure that what I believe is right. I want to be sure that the reward of what I have chosen is worth the potential negative outcome. I don't want to live my life poorly to find out that there is a major unknown consequence awaiting me.

We also have to consider how strongly we believe. To use an old wartime analogy, "is this the hill you are willing to die on?" Is your belief worth suffering the ultimate consequence? If yes, congratulations, you have arrived. If not, why not? The answers to these questions will either convict you in your beliefs or send you further on your quest.

We have determined that if there is a God and he has rules, we should be able to find out what they are here and now before we get thrust into an area of consequences. If there are rules, either implicit or explicit, then they must be findable and definable so we can know how to properly live our lives. If we can know how to properly live our lives we can know what is improper and know the consequences for that impropriety.

A look at cultures around the world will show commonalities in the things that are right and wrong. If those things are common, even in cultures that haven't interacted, then that points to a shared moral compass. That commonality points to someone or something that has given us a common point of reference. We then have an obligation to follow that compass. We also have the right to choose. We don't have to take on that obligation; in fact, we don't even have to agree that the obligation exists. When we make our choices we can expect rewards for decisions that follow the rules and consequences for decisions that don't.

We first must establish what the rules are, who the rules come from, and be certain that our foundational work in this area is strong. As we seek the truth we have to establish the baseline of that truth. When people get a hold of partial truths, then embellish those truths for their purposes, the baseline gets lost.

For example, there is a cactus that is common in many areas of several of the deserts of the southwest called the Cholla. There are many varieties of this plant but the one most talked about is the Jumping Cactus. This cactus is hard to describe if you haven't seen it but let me try. Picture a sausage with tooth-picks fairly evenly spaced protruding from the link. When this sausage is set down on your plate the meat doesn't touch the plate, only the points of the tooth picks do. If you pick it up by a tooth pick and set it back down in a different position the sausage will still be suspended and the segment will be held aloft by the tooth picks. That's what a segment of the cholla cactus looks like. The green part of the plant has that sausage shape and it is covered by very sharp spines that protrude evenly around the cactus segment. If it comes into contact with your clothes or your skin the needle like spines will attach to you and the easily dislodged segment will detach from the plant for a ride. This isn't very pleasant but the real trouble starts when you try to remove it. It has sharp spines pointing in every direction so if you grab it with your hand it will attach to your skin there. You now have a very painful situation that isn't easily resolved.

Remember this interesting plant is called a "Jumping Cactus". Knowing that truth, how does that make you feel about going for a hike in the desert? Doing some research might give you more perspective on whether or not you want to go visit the desert so I will give you what I know. I was on a nature walk at an Arizona state park years ago and the "Naturalist", who introduced himself as Jack, described his background as one of a cowboy. He had spent most of his life riding and working in the desert and he learned about the plants and animals from those years of experience. He talked about all the major plants on the nature trail but he gave special attention to the one known as the Jumping Cactus. He told us to keep back from it because it would jump and attach itself to you if you got too close. I don't recall him saying why this plant had this adaptation but the crowd was in awe and everyone moved to the side of the trail as we went past to avoid the cactus.

Over the years I have heard many explanations for how the cactus functions. Most of its seeds are sterile so it does it best reproduction by having the dislodged segments moved to different locations by roaming cow, deer and hikers. So it has a reason for needing to dislodge from the mother plant and attach to passing mammals. Some say that it is static electricity that causes the segments to jump; others say that the joints fall randomly from the plant and the long limber spines help the joints bounce as a way of attachment.

Neither one of these explanations, though, answer what happened once on a hike I was on. I was a tail guide with a group of eight guests on a trail in Saguaro National park. My co-guide who was leading the group was Charlie. We were moving at a good clip when Charlie stopped the group and took off his hat. When I caught up with him he was scratching his head and showing the group a segment of cholla that was stuck in the top of his hat. Everyone looked around but there were no cholla in the immediate area. I had seen some back by me when Charlie first stopped but I had to agree that there were none near by, and certainly none that were towering above our heads. Charlie wondered out loud how this might have happened but none of our guests were able to shed any light on the situation. The legend of the Jumping Cactus is now set to explode in the lives of the hikers and anyone who listens to their stories of the desert adventure they were on.

Oh, by the way, I left out a couple of details. I didn't want to taint the story too early with my perspective, in this case with the rest of the truth. The fact of the matter is that the Jumping Cactus doesn't jump. The accounts above are true. None of the facts are altered except that I left out my personal point of view as a witness to the accounts. I happen to have spent a lot of time in the desert and my passion was to learn as much as I could about the plants and animals, kind of like Jack. I loved to learn and then to pass on the information to others. I went on the hike with Jack because a friend of mine who worked at the park said that he told stories to the park visitor but never let them know that they were stories. We didn't know if he believed them himself or if he was just messing with the tourists so I went on a hike with him to see if I could figure him out.

During the time he was going on about the Jumping Cactus I stepped off of the trail behind him and as he was saying "If you get too close the cactus will jump on you" I was putting my hands near the plant and gently touching the spines to show that what he was saying didn't happen. I didn't want to call him out in front of the group but I didn't want the folks to go home with that lie about the cactus in their brains either. The troubling thing for me was that some of the people who saw me do that had the look of disdain in their eyes as though they felt sorry for me and that I was someday going to end up just covered in the cactus because I wasn't listening to the expert.

On the hike with Charlie I was talking to the man in front of me. As we were moving and while he was making a point he looked over his shoulder to be better heard and in so doing his hand touched a segment of a cholla cactus. His hand reflexively twitched at the sensation and he flicked the piece of cactus up and forward and it landed on Charlie's hat.

When we caught up with Charlie, a man who knows that cholla can't jump, the group had no way of knowing what had happened. Even the man whose action caused the incident had no knowledge of having touched the cactus. When I told my version of the story he couldn't corroborate it. He didn't recall the sensation of touching the cholla or the flick of his hand.

These are the things that we must guard against when we seek the truth. One is someone in authority, like the naturalist, who gives us information that we trust because of who it came from so we don't double check it. The other is incomplete information that arrives against something we know to be true. Charlie knew that cholla doesn't jump but he said if I hadn't seen the incident he would be hard pressed to explain how it happened. Even with my eyewitness account it was a long shot that what I said happened had actually happened. In both of these stories people walked away not fully believing the truth. I'm certain that people on the nature walk and people on the hike tell stories about the jumping cactus and how it will jump and attach itself to you.

Can the story of the jumping cactus have more than one truth? It depends upon your perspective. In chapter 2 we talked about the differences that can occur between our truth and The Truth. To some people it is well established in their mind that the cholla cactus can jump. No matter what the biological truth is they will tell their friends at parties about this strange and wonderful plant. It is the responsibility of the listener to listen with respect, ask some questions and do more research. I would want to know how they knew this to be true. If their answer was "a cowboy naturalist told me so" I would file the information away and find other sources that confirmed or denied that statement.

So the truth from the perspective of the guy at the party is that the cactus can jump. The ultimate truth from the perspective of all the facts being recovered, is that the cactus can not jump on it own accord. If you were on a T.V. game show and the correct answer to that question would win you loads of cash and prizes whose truth would you want to rely on?

The quest for spiritual truth often ends when we hear a "truth" from a perspective that lines up with what we want to be true and feel comfortable with so we put aside any search for back up to that truth. People continually give out information from a position of authority that is incomplete or wrong. Whether they are deliberately trying to mislead or truly believe what they teach doesn't really matter here. Their responsibility is great.

When teachers speak they have an obligation to speak truthfully and use the rulebook effectively so that the students of that belief have some assurance that what they are learning from that teacher is true. When the teacher expresses an opinion he is obligated to state it as such. We, as students and seekers, have the obligation to ferret out the corroboration to verify what we are taught.

I had a talk with several spiritual leaders who were offended that I would talk about the possibility of evil within the spiritual realm. I was surprised as I listened to their reasons for their opposition. They said that the spiritual world was pure and was always good and right. That belief was strong within their context and I found as I tried to make my point as to why I thought the probability of darkness existed they seemed to get even angrier with me. The irony for me was this was from a group who taught a non-judgmental based philosophy. Our discussion remained friendly but their adamant stand on that concept scared me.

If there is such a thing as truth there has to be its opposite. (Remember the discussion on contrast in chapter 4.) As I seek spiritual truth I'm going to assume that there may be entities out there that would rather I didn't find them. They might find a way to blend aspects of the truth with non truth in order to lead me off the path. That is spiritual camouflage (See Chapter 8). If I can convince you that all is good then I can be cuddling with you, with your permission, and still be misguiding you.

To simplify, if we believe that something can be true then we have to believe that something can be false. The only other option would be something like what the above spiritual leaders believed. "All is true and all is good". But, if "all is true" so is my statement that "Falsehood exists". So if all is true and all is good then falsehood is true and good. I have a hard time with that.

Truth exists and so does its opposite. When it comes to spiritual belief is there only one truth that we must follow? Is there a possibility of following something that is false? Consider all of the belief systems across the world. All cultures have a defined spiritual practice. Nearly all of them believe in a God or gods. What does that say to your right brain?

One thought and a strong probability is that there is a common origin for a belief in God. We have cultural variations that may be explained by people wanting to serve a god but not wanting some of the moral or philosophical restrictions placed on them by that god. So they make adjustments to help them keep control of the rules of their god, and to help them be free to do the things they want to do.

That's called changing the rule book.

If truth exists there must be an ultimate truth. If the spiritual realm exists there must be an ultimate spirit. If the concept of God is true there must be an ultimate God. When I consciously set out on my spiritual quest that ultimate God was the being I was looking for. The question for me was "How do I recognize Him and how do I avoid following something less?

If we follow without double checking we will be following down a wrong path.

Can there be more than one truth? I say no if we are talking about truth in the ultimate sense. The truth of the matter is that you should not trust me on this issue. You need to use this topic, as a base from which to do your own research, until you are satisfied with the answer.

Next we will cover how our focus might be swayed away from The Truth.

8.

SPIRITUAL CAMOUFLAGE

If there were a true and singular God what would keep us from knowing Him as such?

If you compare world religions you will find there are so many concepts that they hold in common. At least superficially. If we search with a deeper probe we find that within those similarities they are really deeply contrasted and diametrically opposed in their essential doctrines. If Islam says there is only one god and Hinduism says that there are numerous gods even if they both profess "love each other" they can never be reconciled in their essential doctrine. In this case we see again that either one is right and the other is wrong or they both are wrong. So if there is the possibility of a doctrine being incorrect how do we justify so many people following that doctrine? How could so many people be mislead? In this quest it boils down to spiritual camouflage.

Camouflage is defined in part as "any disguise; false pretense." If there is only one truth and you have to follow it to succeed all I have to do, as your opposition, is to get you on a distorted path and I have achieved my goal. In this case, my job would be to convince you that all world religions teach the same basic principals so they all do the same thing. How do I best accomplish this act of misleading you? With camouflage. Let's take an example from the physical world.

To be successful I need to find a way to blend in; I need to fit into your landscape so that you don't even notice my existence or my intent. On September 11th, 2001 an organized group of people were able to pull off an act of terrorism, on U.S. soil, that came out of nowhere to most American people. The terrorists' boarded several commercial aircraft, took control of the planes and then proceeded to crash them into select targets including the twin towers of the World Trade Center in New York and the Pentagon in Washington D.C.

How were a handful of people able to infiltrate our system and wreak such havoc? They blended in. They lived their lives so that the people around them wouldn't see them as bad or suspicious people. People saw them day to day and their story was one of conformity to the local's daily lives. They didn't stand out so they were not even noticed until they accomplished what they wanted to do. Looking back we can put together the evidence and tie in all of the details of what they were doing in our presence but at the time they blended in without arousing suspicion.

That was all done on a physical level but it has a great lesson to teach in the study of spiritual things as well. If I were the one in charge of being sure you didn't find spiritual truth and I wanted to misguide you I would be sure to let you believe that everything was fine; that everything that you believed spiritually was in line with what others believed; and that if you look at all of the world religions you'd see that they have so many things in common that one can't possibly be the only way. My plan would be to show you the similarities mentioned earlier so that you would not feel a need to probe deeper. I'd be sure that you didn't care about the differences.

I believe the doctrine of Christianity, when it follows the essentials, is the one true way to eternity with God. I know that this claim can be very offensive to people so I would ask you to follow along with an open mind and see how this Truth develops.

After years of being offended by such a line as "there is only one way to God" I started to notice some things. Whenever I was with a group of people who discussed their spiritual beliefs there seemed to only be an offense when someone confessed the Christian faith. I saw people who followed the spiritual ways of the Hindu, the Buddhist, the Native American and even the Jew, which is the foundation of Christian belief, welcomed into the conversation but if someone said "I am a Christian" the walls went up. It was all right to say that you believed in God but not to say that you believed in Jesus Christ as God. This intrigued me. My law enforcement mind detected evidence of someone trying to hide something. I just didn't know whom. Or what. So I watched and waited. I didn't believe this religion was true but I was still interested in how it was playing out.

As a Ranger in state and national parks part of my job was to be on the look out for people doing things that were against the laws and rules of the park. As my partner and I would drive or walk through a portion of the park there was an action that usually gave us a big hint that someone was doing something wrong. In training it was called furtive movement.

As we were moving through a picnic area during the annual springtime alcohol ban in the park we would come upon a group of young adults who were talking, laughing and generally doing what people do in such areas. Then someone in the group would see us walking their way and there would be a sudden change in the individual's actions. Then whole group would follow suit.

The classic example would be that the one who saw us would take whatever was in their hand lean quickly over toward the ground then sit back up with hands neatly folded in front of them and stare straight ahead. Sometimes we would see his lips moving and then a sudden burst of either loads of furtive activity or a complete change in behavior from having fun to serious and quiet.

Seeing how we weren't known for being evil and mean when it came to our contacts we would always know there was something to investigate at the table. It was our cue to go over and say howdy. Typically we would find that the one who had started the process had an ice cold beer sitting on the ground next the to picnic table leg closest to him.

The point is that when everything seems to be going normally and there is a sudden change in program it is time to check out the area for possible reason why.

The people at the table were trying to hide something, to camouflage their activity. They wanted to do what wasn't supposed to be done and not have anyone outside of their group know it. At first I was offended that people would even try to break the rules but later my attitude changed. I knew that people would try and I started to enjoy and admire those who had some creativity in the process. Knowing that some would try to get away with breaking the law I looked forward to those who would offer up a bit of a challenge in their process.

When it comes to physical camouflage the people I admire most are the Apache of the Southwestern U.S. I read the stories of Cochise and Geronimo, both Chirichauan Apache leaders. They were able to lead their people across the deserts and avoid detection even when over 4000 U.S. and Mexican soldiers were assigned to capture or kill them. They knew the landscape and had mastered the techniques of blending in.

One account of a survivor of an Apache attack tells of how his regiment was riding through the desert among small shrubs and large rocks when the large rocks suddenly became Apaches. Those men had mastered the art of camouflage so well that they were perceived as part of the landscape. I admire the physical ability of those Apache and what they were able to do with it. That sort of ability is useful in the spiritual realm as well.

Earlier we established that if good exists then so to does evil. That dark side of the Christian walk is known as Satan. In the physical world I admire the Apache's for their abilities in guerilla warfare. In the spiritual realm I have a similar admiration for Satan. (Two things before I go on. I don't equate the Apaches with devils and I do not look upon the ability of Satan with love. Just as we all admire a good opponent in a competitive sport because of their ability to outwit us at times, our goal is still to come out on top at the end of the competition. I see Satan as a worthy opponent that I have to respect and who I cannot beat without major help.) I know the goal of the Christian walk, to believe in the essential doctrine and to tell others with love, gentleness and respect about why I follow that doctrine. I also know the goal of the other side, to make my point of view look foolish or unreasonable and to present an option that looks and feels better to the one considering the options.

The Bible states that the goal of the successful Christian path is through a narrow gate, it is defined as such by the founder of the faith. Satan, because he is a worthy opponent, knows that as well. And because all that has to happen for him to win is to nudge you off the difficult path before you get to the narrow gate, he has the upper hand early in the game. We start out his quest as a soccer team without a goalie. Without diligent study we are at a serious disadvantage. Think of all the choices we have when choosing a spiritual world view. Here is a partial list: Hinduism, Buddhism, Judaism, Christianity, Atheism, Confucianism, Islam, Taoism, Voodoo, Paganism and so on. It's like being in the world's largest candy store with more choices that you can imagine and then I come along and tell you that you must choose only one. And I'm going to tell you which one is best. That will cause some conflict.

So as the opposing team my job is simple. I employ a gentle nudge to make you wander off the path. The troubling part is that when we go, we go willingly either by deliberate choice or by lack of study.

So what would my tactics be if I had the job of Satan? I'd be sure that I was misrepresented as a creature that was big, mean, ugly and obvious. I'd want you to think that you could see me coming a mile away. What is the image in your head now of the devil? Is he a character in a red suit with horns, a pointed tail and a 3 pronged pitchfork? If I was his public relations guy and that is the image in your head I have done my job well. What most people have in their mind is a cartoon character (Not really dangerous) who you will see coming (so you can relax) and who probably sits on your left shoulder as your angel sits on your right. The one on the right always wins so, Whew! We don't have anything to worry about.

The true entity behind the cartoon is described in 2 Corinthians 11:14 as a being who "transforms himself into an angel of light." It is the perfect camouflage. You are expecting a highly visible, and identifiable as evil character, but he wanders in as a gentle thing that you feel you can trust. Think about a time that you willingly did something wrong. If you are like me you rationalized why it would be all right for you to do. You probably even had some corroboration near you that the rationalization made complete sense. There was numbness to the potential consequences of doing whatever it was and you did the thing. Afterward there was the hurt, embarrassment, guilt, loss, etc. That is what Satan really looks like, both in the first and second phase of his process.

When studying all of the options how do we respond to all of the choices and, in particular, to the choice that I offered you that offends most that are presented with it? It is at this point that we tend to accept the premise that the world is filled with gray.

Early in my serious quest I started to use my Law enforcement thought process to examine what I knew about my thoughts and reactions to the religious beliefs that had been presented to me.

When it comes to the Ford versus Chevy or Coke versus Pepsi debate we are typically very comfortable with having, and accepting from others, a black and white argument. If you like Ford you have your reasons and that white point of view is what you defend. You expect the opposition to hold to their black point of view in a similar fashion even as you argue that they are completely wrong.

This is typical until one gets to the discussion of religion. At that point there is a shift to gray. A furtive movement. Everything is going along normally then the subject of religion comes up and anyone who has a black and white view is suspect. I went through this process myself and eventually started to feel the same gnawing I felt when I saw the furtive movement at the park's picnic table. Why wouldn't I, or others around me, accept a black and white position from someone else in this conversation when we would if it was a conversation about chicken or beef? The deeper I thought about and researched it the more I realized that the first discussion was mundane and the second one might have long-lasting effects. It was the furtive movement that bothered me.

What I observed was a consistent acceptance of everything but the most vile, (Satanism with blood sacrifices) or the doctrine of Christ. Since I knew that the teachings of the man Jesus were ones of love and acceptance and that most world religions agreed he existed, I was intrigued by the dichotomy. The most common reason for denying Christian belief was that it claims to be an exclusive route to God and no loving God would demand such a limit. What struck me was that if I were Christ and wanted to gain acceptance to my way of thinking, why would I use such a limiting tactic? Any human would know that such a limiting belief system would likely have few followers. If I personally wanted to start a church I know, to draw a crowd, I'd have to offer a host of options. Why would Christ, God in human flesh, make such limits and expect followers? He is either delusional or what he offered is true in its precision. If I wanted to counter a truth with such limitations, what better tactic than to offer any other, more broad, solution? I'd say, "Follow me. I offer happiness with no real commitment, no real expectations and no real work on your part."

Though this book doesn't allow for an exhaustive study keep in mind that Christianity (including its Jewish foundation) is the only historic faith. The people and the places of the Old and New testaments have been clearly documented through the works of archeologist. The Bible is not a science manual but it records scientific facts long before the discipline of science was commonly in use. No other belief system can claim these things. Not even those who believe in Darwinism. It is becoming more evident, according to the comments of even secular scientists that there is less science in the theory of evolution than there is in the concept of a biblical God. The more science learns the more believable the Bible becomes. Christ was the only founder of a world religion who claimed to be God. That by itself could be a reason to walk away from the doctrine except that the whole bible, 66 books, written by over 40 people over a span of 1500 years points to the coming of, and the redemption promised by, Christ. If it is a conspiracy it has been perpetuated by a bunch of folks who never met and who passed it on over the centuries without a glitch. That gives it a solid internal integrity. I think of the Watergate cover-up during the Nixon presidency, and how quickly that fell apart, and I find it impossible to believe that a 1500 year old conspiracy could happen.

Christ stated that "narrow is gate and difficult is the way that leads to life, and there are few who find it." (Matthew 7:14). If that is true and I wanted to lead you astray, all I would have to do is appeal to your independent nature, and lead you to believe that such a saying could not be accurate because of its narrow scope. (Think of how that passage affects you now. Everyone has a right to be offended but my cop's mind would ask "What is the real reason for the feeling? Do you respond or react? Is the statement that far off or is there some part of it that resonates with you and that is the cause of your offense?") If I could do that, working as Satan, I would have infiltrated your world, with your permission, and accomplished my goal of nudging you off the path. The good news for me is that a nudge is all that is required. I don't have to bowl you over just put you on the outside edge of the path so you miss the "narrow gate".

What is most likely to be camouflage; a moral and limited rule based belief system with rewards for all good deeds and punishments for all bad ones, which most people are offended by; or a worldview that we all are OK and you can do as you please and so can I and we all live happily ever after? One requires of us a self-discipline that is hard to sit with. The other requires that we go about our merry way without accountability. We tend to want the latter for ourselves but close examination would reveal that from others we want the former.

When I think of spiritual distraction I go back to my days as a ranger. The best cops are those who understand the bad guys and the way they work. If I were to be put in charge of distracting you from the truth I would do exactly what seems to be going on in the spiritual debate today.

I think of a game I once played in a mountain biking workshop. Two orange cones were set up at the far end of a field and two bicyclists rode toward them. The object of the game was to go between the cones while preventing the other rider from doing the same. The riders had to stay in contact, shoulder to shoulder, all the way down the field and the best technique was to wait until the last minute then make your move. The one to apply the right amount of pressure at the right moment won the point. Because narrow is the gate to winning, all that was required was the right nudge to stop the opponent from success. The biggest player didn't always win. More often it was the one who camouflaged their technique, allowing the other player to believe it was going to be easy to prevail, and at the last second making the decisive move.

Now, what if my object was not to gain points for myself, according to the rules you understood, but to only prevent you from getting any points for yourself? I could lean hard against you but let you push me away from the center of the course. I would let you think you were winning, but just barely, and then at the last second I would lean away from you causing your weight to propel you away from the goal. I would miss the gate by a lot and you would miss it by a little. I obtain my objective because you missed the gate.

I camouflaged my intent. You assumed I needed a point but I really don't care about my points. I only care that you don't get any. When we both crossed the line without a point, I won. "Not fair", you say? To me that is an example of a most effective camouflage. Historically speaking the one who wants to prevent you from finding this spiritual truth is not concerned about gaining these sorts of points. He is only concerned that you believe that he is, and then he sets out to prevent you from gaining critical points for yourself.

As I study belief systems and worldviews the ones that concern me aren't the ones that restrict me in logical ways. The narrow path makes sense to me. Every action has attached to it either a reward or a consequence. That is how we work as parents and business leaders and the philosophy makes sense. The systems that concern me are the ones that allow me nearly total freedom. When someone tells me that I can do whatever I want without concern, I get concerned.

Think about it. If one looks at the concept of moral law objectively most humans will agree on some basic concepts. From culture to culture all will agree that certain things are repulsive: Rape, murder, theft. Even a professional thief gets offended when something of his is stolen. Where do these beliefs come from? Some would say that society defines these things and rules and cultures vary. It must be agreed that there is variance from society to society but even where there is a predominance of abuses the only ones who agree that this behavior is acceptable are the ones who have a selfish benefit to gain from the behavior. An example can be taken from cultures where men completely dominate women and the most subtle infraction of the men's law by the women will result in her beating or her death. The men say this is as it should be; the women, and the people of most other cultures, disagree and find it appalling. Looking at it from the standard of moral law who is right?

The scientific rule of cause and effect states that one cannot create something that is greater than oneself. This moral standard, so easily broken by us with our rationalization, has to then come from a source greater than ourselves. We can justify the breaking of the standard with our selfish wants and desires but when put to the test in the still dark night we have a nagging within our heart that tells us we are doing something wrong. We then try to wash away that nagging with our rationalization. It gets further washed away with repeated violation of the rule and the consequent feeling of power and the control that results. But until the very end there will always be a seed of the truth that it is wrong buried within our conscience. That deep understanding within our consciousness doesn't come from the man made laws of society. Those laws are formed because something morally greater than us has put those laws within us. The laws we create for our society are based on that common internal source. If that source is "common" all people have it and that indicates it originates from a single source.

In recent times the line that divides all the potential sources of such morality has become blurred. I took a class not long ago where, during the lesson, the instructor referred to an entity by many names. His apparent intent was to make a point about our creativity and where it comes from without offending anyone in the audience. He said that to open up our left brain flow we need to be receptive to a source outside ourselves.

Some of the names he gave this spiritual source were Muse, from the Greek, Holy Spirit, from Christianity, Higher Power, from New Age belief and he grouped them all together as The Author Within. The trouble is that in trying to appeal to everyone he clumped entities together that contradict one another.

To the Christian saying that the Holy Spirit and the Muse are the same is offensive. The New Age believer may, or may not, accept Higher Power alongside of the Muse. A Buddhist wouldn't see the need to attach a concept of God to any of this because of the atheistic nature of his faith. Names have a meaning because of the agreements we put behind them. There is a danger in diluting those meanings.

Picture an apple. You have a few varieties to choose from but it is safe to say that you and I are now thinking of the same fruit. We have agreed arbitrarily with our language that the term "apple" denotes a particular fruit. If when I say "here, take this apple." but hand you a pear you will be surprised by the contrast. If I grew up on an isolated English speaking island and had been taught from childhood that what I held in my hand was an apple even though all other English speakers knew it as a pear, would that change the characteristics of the piece of fruit?

We can even change the language and still get the same outcome.

Picture a Manzana. If you don't know the language you may be stumped. If you spoke Spanish and I were bilingual, just recently learning Spanish, you'd have a picture in your head of a Manzana and I would have a picture in my head of an apple. If we did a sketch for a crowd we both would draw a picture of the same fruit. Now, no matter what language the people in the crowd spoke what would come immediately into their minds is their word for "apple".

Now remember, I come from that island where I learned that the word apple describes a pear. If I sketched this fruit in Italy I would be told that it is a pera. Having believed that I learned the word for apple I would go to the market ask for the fruit and be confused when the grocer handed me what he heard me request. I got what I asked for but not what I had intended.

So if I appeal to the Muse for inspiration when I write, but what I really want is help from the Holy Spirit, I am likely to get what I asked for but not what I intended. Or, if I believe all these things to be one and the same I may get answers from places completely unknown to me. This is spiritual camouflage. If I want you to seek general help and not be certain of where that help comes from I will be more than happy to lead you to believe that all those titles belong to one and the same source and anything you ask of any of them will give you a safe and comfortable answer.

If the Holy Spirit is what I seek but I am not fully aware of what that means, I can be mislead. If I come to you as the Buddha, but don't have all the characteristics of the Buddha, I am not the Buddha. Conversely, if I have any characteristics that contradict the Buddha, I am not the Buddha. Where we can be confused is when we don't have a complete understanding of who the Buddha, or the Muse or the Holy Spirit, is.

The example in the class struck me as a way that those not fully educated in their faith might start to be lead in another way.

The Muse may appeal to someone who has studied and admired the culture of the Greeks. The Author Within might appeal to an Atheist. The Higher Power may fit in well with a New Age practitioner. But put together the definitions of these entities contradict each other. The Holy Spirit, in the Christian faith, is God Himself; the Muses are minor gods in the stories of Zeus and company and by definition don't compare. They don't hold the attributes of the Christian God. If Christianity is true and a casual practitioner of that faith called upon a muse without looking to his God, who would answer?

If I were the bad guy I would want to sneak up on you. If I wanted to confuse you and make your faith unproductive I would come to you, as the pear that I am, even though you seek an apple. If you noticed the switch I would do my best to convince you that it is not an apple but a pear that you truly desire.

If you were new to the faith and still unsure of who was who and why, I would have my best opportunity to trip you up. If I wanted to prevent you from staying on that "narrow path" I would come smiling, introduce myself as the Holy Spirit, take your hand and lead you away. If I did my job well you'd grip my hand in affection and follow.

A question that came up for me and should also for you is "How do I know now that this isn't just someone coming smiling to lead me away? Good question. The thoughts and processes in this book are set up so that you can use a logical and scientific approach to establish the truth. How this fits into your quest will be different for you than it was for me. Your epiphany will not be the same as mine. I would encourage you to look deeply into the options before you and "do the math". Because you are a seeker of truth your heart and brain will know, at least subtly, when something is off.

Just remember that 2+2 is always 3. (See how that works?)

9.

WHO DO I ASK ABOUT THE TRUTH?

⋄⇌◎⇋⋄

That is a tough question. As rational people we tend to want sufficient truth about something we are skeptical of before we will accept it. As noted earlier, if we want something to be true then just another person agreeing with us is enough. If we don't agree with a subject, then we need an overwhelming amount of evidence to even consider the option.

It is one thing to believe when you have solid research options, but how do we know for certain about a God who we can't physically see? Here's where the modicum of faith mentioned in the preface comes in. We need to ask Him.

Imagine a scenario where we stand in an art gallery and listen to patrons discussing a piece of artwork. The conversation goes something like this:

"The artist, obviously a genius, has used color here to demonstrate the frailty of the human condition".

"No, no," another replies. "I see the juxtaposition of the key elements of the landscape as symbolism of man's inability to communicate peacefully with one another."

"No way. You obviously have no idea what you are talking about!"

"I'm about to show you how frail *your* condition is!"

If the artist walked up incognito and gave his impression, "It was a lovely spring day, after a long cold winter, and the artist wanted to capture the feeling that overcame him as the warmth of the sun reflected off of the landscape and warmed his heart", he would be pooh-poohed away by those who felt they were in the know. But who better to answer the question of the artist's intent than the artist himself? Even if his answer doesn't fit with your worldview, or your interpretation of the art, it has to be perceived as the truth of the art in question.

It is one thing to ask a physical artist what his works mean and quite another to seek the answers from a non-physical God. How do we hear him? How do we know who really answers? Where is our researchable proof?

If I were standing on the street and needed help with a medical problem whom would I seek to answer my concerns? A doctor, of course. How would I know that the person I talked with was a doctor? One way would be by the knowledge they expressed of the medical concern I was researching. To know this though I would have to have some knowledge of basic medicine to be able to discern the alleged doctors answers. Even when we are with a doctor we have placed our trust in we have occasions when we wish to seek a second opinion. Those times would be when we don't want the truth of what he is saying to be the truth. In that case much more evidence will be needed to even consider the option we oppose.

When on a quest you have to study. You have to look at the rulebooks, understand the contrasts, believe in truth and recognize your presuppositions. You have to guard against the possibility of inaccurate information, either deliberate or not, coming to you. In short you have to go in search of the truth. There is a danger in just hoping that it will come to you without your contribution.

Once you have a foundation from which to ponder new information, the best place to ask about the truth is from the one who created your ability to do this quest in the first place. How can we do that and be sure that the answers that come back to us are from the giver of the ultimate truth? If I ask a medical question anyone can give me their opinion. I certainly don't want the answer from someone who gets all their information on medicine from an internet chat room. I want the answer from a specialist in the particular field of my concern. I would seek to get my answer from a particular person who had the background to give me not just an answer but the complete answer.

When you seek to understand spiritual truth it makes sense to pose your question very specifically.

We are dealing with a source we can't see and that we can't rationally prove exists. So when you lay out the question what are the characteristics of the entity from which you want an answer? I won't presume to know what you would seek here, but let me show you my list to give you a starting point. You don't have to agree with this list but you still can apply the process to match your worldview.

Here is the process I used.

1) If I was created, and science points to that as the most likely scenario, then my creator has to be more than I am. (Remember, the law of cause and effect: we can't create something that is greater than us. Any cause is greater than its effect.) Looking at the creation as a whole with all of its intricacies, details and moral potential, I see the cause of this creation to be very great indeed.

2) If I was created, what was here before me to cause this creation? The creator would have to exist in a different kind of world than I am accustomed to living in. He has to live outside of my space-time continuum. He cannot be seen or touched physically in the space/time continuum in which I live.

3) If I was created, what is the reason, the purpose for my existence? There has to be a plan even if I don't yet know what it is. The creator of this program has full knowledge of what is going on and what I am to do within that program.

4) If He knows all that is suppose to go on here, He must be aware of all that is occurring at all times.

5) If He did all of that, what is his attitude toward me? I think of my attitude toward my children, who I technically didn't create but I did have a part in their coming to be. Even when they frustrate me by not following the rulebook set by my wife and me, I love them. So my creator must love me unconditionally or I wouldn't be able to express that similar sort of love for my kids.

So in my quest for the final answer I thought it through this way. If I was put here by a Creator, that Creator must have all of these attributes as defined by the law of cause and effect. He must be all knowing, all loving, ever-present and all powerful. Possessing those characteristics, if I came to him not knowing but truly searching for the truth, I surmised he would give me the answers to my direct and sincere questions. With that much in mind here is what I did. When my kids came to me with questions about life, I always do my best to answer them to their level of understanding. Knowing and expecting that of myself, I put the same qualifications into the mix for the one from which I sought my answers. If I, as an imperfect human dad, would do my best to correctly answer the questions of my children I would trust that a perfect entity, acting in the position of my creator, would give me perfect answers. I had to be careful that I asked the questions of the right entity. I also needed to be sure that I didn't read too much into the answers. I couldn't try to make them what I wanted instead of what I had asked for.

Here is the formula I used and the reasons why. "God, creator of all things, (This narrowed down the possible sources from which an answer would come) I want to know the truth about Your purpose." (This opened me up to disappointment if the truth wasn't what I wanted it to be but it allowed for only a specific type of answer.) " Show me, in a language that I understand who you are and what my role is in your plan." (This assured I would get the information in the size and condition I needed to be able to digest it.)

Have the answers come? Yes. Have they come as I expected? Sometimes, but not always. Have I received everything I needed to be completely at ease with all of the questions the search for spiritual truth brings up? No, but I chalk that up to the fact that I am not yet ready for some of the information. Patience is a definite requirement for this journey. It is safe to say that things that I interpreted from the early part of my quest have changed in my mind as I progress. Not that the information I received has changed, just the way I look at it, the way I have altered its true meaning.

So I want to be clear on this point. Take what you read here as being presented as the truth as I understand it. Then take that information and objectively double check it. I can not be the ultimate source of anyone's spiritual truth. I think there is only one entity that can be trusted with that. I addressed Him as God, the creator of all things at the beginning of my true quest. So far I have not found that I have been mislead except by my own hand. We only run into trouble when we set the parameters for what truth has to look like for our personal acceptance.

Who do we ask to get truthful answers? Go to the source. What is our risk?

1) Disappointment with an answer when we hope that a particular thing is the truth and we find that it is not.

2) Seeking our answers from sources that will give us a consensus on what we want to believe but being lead away from the real truth.

Seeking, finding and understanding the truth can be hard. Sometimes the answers aren't what we want them to be. Sometimes we hope an answer will make our lives easier but it doesn't. The real question at this point is "Do I really want to know the truth?"

Don't just skim over that question. Understand what you really want that answer to be. We still have the gift of free will. We don't have to look for the truth and if we accidentally stumble upon it we don't have to follow. That gift is both a great blessing and a great burden depending on how it is applied. We know it as the freedom of choice. It is great to say that we have it but along with that freedom we have to consider that all choices have either a reward or a consequence. What do I get in return for not seeking the truth? What do I get for not following something I know to be true? What hardships might I encounter if I do follow the truth but it is not popular? Are there rewards in store for that same scenario?

Think of eating chocolate, or any other sweet favorite of yours. We love the stuff and there is always an immediate reward for its consumption. If we go too far, though, there are areas of consequence such as too many calories, not enough nutrition or blemishes on the face from the indulgence. I don't consider this quest a game, but to use a game analogy, all games have rules. There are the rewards and consequences for following or disobeying those rules. If I stay inbounds on a basketball court I can continue to move toward my team's goal and potentially score. That's a reward. If I step out of bounds the whistle is blown, the ball is taken from me and the other team controls the direction of travel. That's a consequence. How do we apply this to our quest? Surely an all loving creator wouldn't provide a consequence that would be uncomfortable to me would he? As a father I would have to say the answer is yes. If my parents didn't enforce their rules I'd know that I wasn't cared for. Those rules are designed to educate and protect. Without them I probably wouldn't have made it to the point where I could make and enforce rules with my kids. Whether or not they agree with me, they know why I do what I do.

An all-loving creator has put rules in place, whether I agree with them or not, in order to educate and protect me. That's a model I can trust because in every culture the norm is that parents try to do the same sort of thing with their kids. We get that characteristic from someone. I sought out the truth in the way that I did because that is a model I can trust. How will you proceed on your quest? Are you satisfied with the truth you hold? Are there fundamental questions still left unanswered? Are there holes in the fabric of your belief or is everything looking good?

The fabric of truth should have no patches. The quest for spiritual truth may occur in pieces, but the truth, when viewed as a whole, must be seamless. When a hole is found the repair should conform as though there never was a hole in the first place. If your fabric appears to have a patch your quest is not over.

Do you hold to a truth that can't satisfactorily answer questions when someone asks you about what you believe? This doesn't mean you need to know everything all at once. There is a great line in the rulebook of the Christian faith. A man is talking to God and says "Lord, I believe; help my unbelief!" I find this to be a common condition of people on this quest. If we put that request at the feet of the giver of truth then the unbelief will be handled. Not all at once but handled none the less.

I believe that I will be fleshing out the details of my belief for the rest of my life. I'm comfortable doing so because I am certain that I have found the truth. My job is to prove it right or prove it wrong. Every time I set out to prove it wrong I come up with more evidence to solidify my foundation. That, for me is satisfying.

There is a reason this is called a quest. It takes time but the reward is worth the expense. Go slowly and consider everything. If you are seeking your questions from the right source, the truth has to come out.

10.

MY QUEST

I was born into a non-religious family yet I was baptized into the Lutheran Church. My mom felt the duty to do at least that because generations of her family had followed that tradition. I never understood or took part in those beliefs and it wasn't modeled in our household. I went to Sunday school at the local Lutheran church not because of an interest in the teachings but as a way to avoid the hard work required of me and my brother by our stepfather. I learned a bit of the doctrine as required and sang the hymns but I never felt moved.

When I was eleven I went on my first camping trip with a neighbor and I found my calling. I was and still am in love with nature. I have always felt my best when I am outdoors and I have molded a career based on this love.

When the questions of God started to come up in my life they naturally grew from the natural point of view. I still remember the first time that nature really spoke to me. It was a winter afternoon in western Wisconsin. The sun was low, I was alone, and my heart was filled with the joy of being outside. As I was wandering back to my house, treading across a 50 yard long snow drift I felt the cold winter wind like a friend on my back.

Two saplings growing close together were squeaking as they rubbed together in the wind. Any voice from the wilderness, to this day, draws me but this was the first time I noticed that voice. I stood and listened to the foreign language being spoken by the works of nature and wondered what it was trying to tell me. I really didn't know but I felt peaceful and at home and I have listened for that voice ever since.

Prior to that afternoon I had gone through a series of half-hearted attempts to understand the world we lived in, how it came to be and if there could actually be a God.

In school we were taught, from the point of view of science that we had evolved from the swamp from single cell organisms. Vast periods of time had allowed us to develop from simple form to the complex form we now enjoyed. I got this infor-mation from people whom I trusted and who were authorities on such things, so I accepted the infor-mation without question. Though I had heard from the Sunday school teacher that a God did exist, my science teachers declared science was in opposition to that idea. Since science had the process to prove its program it was the one that made the most sense.

The trouble was that I kept hearing this voice from the woods that lead me to believe there was something more out there than just the static rocks and sticks. There was a life force that I couldn't put my finger on but that I could sense. I couldn't prove it to anyone but I knew it so well that no one could prove to me that it wasn't there.

Eventually I combined the two schools of thought so the truths that I held made sense to me. I figured that this unseen thing in the woods was a form of god trying to speak to me and yet I saw the logic in how things could have evolved from a single celled life form. My conclusion was that God created the amoeba and it did the rest. My conflict with my early days in church was fixed. God watched as we evolved from an amoeba into men and if the church people wanted to surmise that Adam and Eve were the first two full humans that still worked.

I spent as much of my time as I could in nature enjoying its effect and trying to understand this unexplainable force of god that I felt there. I used my love of the outdoors and found a job as a park ranger. During those years I had a friend and co-worker who was a Christian. She invited me to her church and, because I was a friend, I agreed to go.

The congregation was strange to me, with people speaking in weird languages during the time of prayer, but I held my tongue for my friend's sake and listened politely to the pastor. I don't recall the message but I remember liking the way it was presented. The man spoke well and I felt his sincerity.

At the end of the service he led the congregation in a final prayer. While we all had our heads bowed he asked for anyone who wanted to accept the gift offered by Jesus Christ to open their eyes and look toward the pulpit. He said he would silently acknowledge our desire and no one else would know. In the passion of the moment I thought that it sounded like a good idea so I lifted my head and opened my eyes. He nodded at me and I went back into the accepted position of prayer.

He finished by saying, "If you accepted Jesus into your heart you must share that decision with someone today."

I thought the decision was going to be a private one and I was embarrassed. I decided that my choice was done in the passion of the moment and I never told anyone of that indiscretion. God wasn't in a stuffy old building, he was in the woods, and I would seek him there.

I spent the next 10 years doing just that. I made my park ranger job a total career choice. While other young men that I worked with used it as a stepping stone to get a job as "a real cop" I chose it for what that job meant for me. Someone was paying me to do what I would do on my day off. I enjoyed the mental work of law enforcement but that was secondary to working outdoors. I worked in the woods and spent my free time in the woods. Over the years I evolved from being a child and not really thinking about God to being an Atheist because of what I had learned in school to feeling a strong draw toward seeking a god that I couldn't fathom but that I knew dwelled in the woods. I found my comfort there and as I became more comfortable being in the wilderness with less gear I turned toward the only belief system that made sense and put it all together for me. I started to study and practice Native American spiritual beliefs. My world was filled with people who practiced the same sort of religion and the more I trained in wilderness schools the more people I met that I could relate to. I thought often of the first time the trees had talked to me that afternoon in Wisconsin. I knew that I was now following the proper path for understanding God.

When I was 24 I developed diabetes. It was not directly life threatening but it was chronic and it hindered my being in the woods. I wanted to be able to walk into a wilderness area with no gear but the disease required that I always carry my insulin, syringes and some food to counter-act insulin reactions. I wanted to find a way to be rid of this disease and I had learned from one of my wilderness skills teachers that all physical ailments were merely caused by "dis-ease" in our harmony with nature. I started to seek out away to remove the symptoms of this "dis-ease".

During this time I got married and in the days before the wedding I reconnected with a high school friend who came to Arizona for the celebration. Jerry, another friend Tom, and I went to Nevada as part of my bachelor party and enjoyed each others company as we had in high school. In school I enjoyed messing with Jerry's head. We would get into a debate about a topic and I would argue my point until he gave in. Then, for fun, once I had convinced him that I was right I would turn the topic back to the argument he was making and work to change his mind again. It was always easy to do this to him and he never held it against me. Tom and I figured just for old time's sake we might mess with him on the trip to Nevada. We spent our time catching up on what we had been doing over the years and telling stories of our glory days.

On the way back from Nevada I asked Jerry, "Are you still listening to that long-haired, hippie-freak, communist, rock and roll music?"

"Nope", he said.

I was glad that maybe he had finally started to listen to the stuff that I liked.

"What are you listening to now?"

"Contemporary Christian music."

I thought now was the time to mess with his head. For the next several hundred miles we talked on and off about his recent conversion to Christianity. I didn't like the message it held but I had to admit it was the first time that he had the ability to counter all of my questions and doubts without faltering. The conversation turned into a serious discussion about our beliefs and not an occasion for me to mess with him. When I tried he always had an answer that stopped me.

After my wedding, my wife Susan and I moved to my home state of Wisconsin. While I was there I finally connected with a medicine man that would help me with my diabetes. The path to meeting him was long and filled with "coincidences". I was given an article about a man named Gilbert during my search and it gave me a way to contact him on the Pine Ridge Reservation in South Dakota.

When I called Gilbert I found that he was a medicine man who practiced a method called Yuwipi. It literally means "they untie him". He told me what to expect and invited me out to his land on the Pine Ridge Reservation. This was what I had been waiting for. Not only was I assured that I could be healed of my diabetes but I was finally going to sit at the feet of a man who really practiced the religion that I had chosen. It was hard for a white man to find a native teacher on the reservation so I was hoping to learn much from my time with Gilbert.

I had discovered that I loved being in the woods and that I felt God must be there but He never contacted me directly. It was in a ceremony with Gilbert that I finally had actual contact with the spirit world.

I spent several days at Gilbert's and his apprentice, Tony, taught me what to expect and how to properly prepare for these ceremonies. It was tradition to offer the medicine man a Canupa, the sacred pipe, when asking for a ceremony. He would then smoke the pipe and seek the answer from the spirits on how to proceed. Being that Gilbert worked with the white population, he allowed that Tony would fill the pipe he used for just this occasion so that those who came and didn't have a pipe to offer could still seek a healing. I did the preparations and Tony presented the pipe to Gilbert on my behalf and I waited for the response.

Another man was there in the middle of his ceremony and I was able to participate. We did a powerful sweat lodge and later that night I witnessed my first Yuwipi ceremony. Tony had told me what to expect in a Yuwipi and the answer of what I was to do for my healing was to come at this event so I was excited. When we entered the room in the old building that was used for the ceremony everything had been set up. The floor at the center of the room was filled with sage which is a sacred herb used by the Lakota. At the north end of the altar area there was a mound of dirt, some rawhide rattles and an eagle bone whistle. All of these were placed there for the use of the Tunkashilas, the grandfather spirits, who would come into the room during the ceremony. Part of the preparation for Gilbert's part was that he was to be tied up in a specific way with a blanket and rawhide cord and laid face down on the bed of sage. The Yuwipi gets it name because during the ceremony the spirits untie the medicine man as part of the process. This particular night Gilbert didn't get tied up and the things I was lead to believe would happen, didn't. Later I was told it was because the man seeking the healing had decided that he wasn't willing to what was expected of him by the spirits.

According to the spirits I was to do a sweat lodge and one night of healing ceremony and I would be healed. Considering that the possibility was up to 4 nights of vision quest and up to 4 nights of healing ceremony I felt that I had an easy time of it. I was given my instructions on how to proceed and so the next day I began my preparations for my healing.

Preparation for that night included that I make a string of 405 prayer ties, 1 inch squares of colored cloth filled with a pinch of tobacco and tied onto a continual piece of string, another string of 75 ties and yet another of 50. I needed to make 7 prayer flags, the same arrangement as the ties only much bigger, to honor the seven directions. (These sacred directions are North, East, South, West, Father Sky, Mother Earth and the direction that points within.) And finally I had to prepare the meal for all the participants of the ceremony. It took me all day and part way into the night to complete.

When all was finished we did a sweat lodge ceremony then headed to the Yuwipi room. This night was to be a full ceremony and the room was filled, around its outer edge, with several people. Members of Gilbert's family who had helped me during the week, his brother, who lead the ceremonial songs, Tony and 3 people who had arrived just to have a minor ceremony done and who participated in my Yuwipi. All were welcome because the more support I had the better my chances for success. Gilbert was tied with a rawhide cord with his hands behind his back. A star quilt was placed over his head and more rawhide cord was used to tie the quilt around him with 7 knots as is the tradition. As the name of the ceremony suggests, when it is over the spirits untie Gilbert leaving the cords in a pile on the altar.

The lights were put out and the drummer and singers began the spirit calling songs. Soon I heard the expected thuds on the floor announcing the arrival of the Tunkashilas. I was told, by Gilbert's brother, to stand and when I did I heard the whistles and the rattles move all around the room. They were moving too fast to be controlled by the people in the room and the belief is that it is the spirits doing what they do in ceremony. Gilbert's brother told me to put my right arm up and as I did the rattles began to touch me. The expectation is that the spirits will assess the patient to do what ever healing is necessary. I knew all of this but I couldn't really believe it.

During this part of the ceremony I leaned back against the wall and tried to see if someone from the room was doing the rattle thing. I felt no one but my doubt was in place. Soon the ceremony ended and we lit the lanterns so we could eat the meal. During the ceremony Gilbert communicates with the Tunkashilas only in the Lakota language. While we were eating the translation was given to me. I was to do 1 night of vision quest and 1 night of healing. I was disappointed. I had entered the ceremony thinking this night was it but now I had a new assignment. I wanted to ask Gilbert why what the spirits had said the night before had changed but I just accepted the new answer and began to prepare. I thought back to my doubt in the ceremony and realized I had to redeem myself.

Gilbert told me I had up to a year to finish up the ceremony. I didn't have the blankets I would need to sit on the vision quest hill in the fall so I made arrangements to finish up in the spring and I went home.

In May my wife and I traveled back to South Dakota and began the interesting part of my quest. Though arrangements had been made for us to be there, when we arrived at Gilbert's place he was nowhere to be found. I contacted his daughter in town and she told me that he had been called away to Massachusetts to do a ceremony. When I called him he said he had tried to call me but must have had the wrong number. I was invited to come out to Massachusetts to finish up but I couldn't afford the time or the expense so we planned on rescheduling for later.

My wife and I decided to visit my friend Jerry, who lived in Rapid City, then go camping for a few days. Before we left Gilbert's daughters home she told me that her uncle, who had helped me in my first ceremony, had died in a car accident this past winter so I thought it fitting to go to a sacred area and offer up prayers on his behalf and to seek direction on what I should do next.

After we checked into a hotel and made plans to have dinner with Jerry and his family we went to Bear Butte, which has been a sacred sight for the Lakota for centuries. I took the traditional prayer ties, pieces of cloth with tobacco tied inside, and sat up on the butte and prayed. I remembered Gilbert's brother and asked for a hint of the direction I should follow next.

While on the mountain I had a vision. I saw a Golden Eagle, a very sacred bird in the Lakota tradition, flying across the sky above my head. As it passed over it turned into a Bald Eagle and flew away. I got up from the sitting area and walked down the butte. I wasn't sure what it meant but I knew I had something to look for. The fact that I had a direct prayer answered in a way that I felt I would be able to interpret was exciting. I had been taught that it was improper to reveal a personal vision to others so I didn't tell my wife what I had experienced but it was on my mind for the rest of that day.

That night we went to have dinner with Jerry and his family at their home.

Whenever Jerry and I got together, or talked on the phone, we talked of spiritual things. He always asked me how my search was going and he always talked to me about his faith. These conversations were usually very long and when we were on the phone one or the other of our wives had to threaten physical violence to get us to hang up to avoid bankruptcy because of the phone bill. After dinner we went to the living room and he played some Christian music for me mainly to show off the sound quality of his stereo. I was happy for the distraction because I wasn't ready to talk about my day with Jerry.

While listening to the music, and the quality of the sound, I noticed matching lamps in the room. They were made from golden wood and carved into the wood was the image of an eagle. I thought of my vision but said nothing. These were Golden Eagles but no Bald Eagles were in sight. Besides I wasn't expecting any answers to my vision being indoors and surrounded by the music.

Later that evening when Jerry was trying to find something to show me near the front of the room I looked at one of the lamps again. Though made from golden wood the image carved on the lamp was actually that of a Bald Eagle. My perceived Golden Eagle had just changed into a Bald Eagle.

It didn't make any sense to me. What could this mean? I figured that I was still moving in the right direction and it must mean that I needed to continue the studies that I came to South Dakota for.

"Good", I thought. "This is the road I want to follow." Sometimes free will can be a burden.

I didn't tell Jerry about this until months later. That hesitancy to talk about it, I later realized, was my fear that my way was not really the proper path. My furtive movement detector went up and I deliberately suppressed it. When I let Jerry in on that coincidence he couldn't understand why I didn't see it as he did. It was a direct answer to my prayer and a path to follow.

"Not even close", I said, and I knew I wasn't rationalizing. I believed that the vision of Bear Butte would reveal itself to me in the nature based way that I expected and needed it to. So I waited.

I continued to seek my healing and spiritual education through Gilbert and the ways of the Lakota. Gilbert traveled a lot doing ceremonies for those who requested them and we lost touch for quite some time. I was excited when he finally called but then a bit disappointed when he was calling to ask for money. I knew that he did all of his work for donations and that many people felt that if they gave him a pack of cigarettes it fulfilled the traditional payment of tobacco. The trouble was that those sorts of gifts didn't feed the family or put fuel into a car. In the end I didn't mind helping him out. He never pressed me and was always genuinely thankful for anything I could do.

Not long after that call he invited me to California to "finish up" my healing. I was told that things would be set up by my arrival but just before I left I was asked for funds to build a Yuwipi room. I didn't have the money or the desire to send it and Gilbert said, "Come anyway. We'll make it happen".

When I got there I was told that a full Yuwipi wasn't going to be possible but I was to prepare all of the items just as I would for that ceremony. So I went off to a private spot and made the required 7 flags and 530 tobacco ties and retuned for the ceremony. It was decided that we would do a Sweat Lodge and Gilbert said I was to ask the Tunkashilas for a healing stone. I was instructed to make a small nest of sage and place it by the door at the east side of the lodge near the pit used for the hot stones. If my prayers were heartfelt and my belief strong the spirits would present me with a stone that would be used as a safety charm for me and to heal my blood relatives if necessary.

I really needed something to bolster my faith so I prayed diligently and with humility but I felt awkward. My heart was guarded and I was not sure this was going to work. Even if it did it was not the ceremony I had come to complete. After the ceremony I was told to crawl to the front of the lodge and retrieve the nest of sage and return to my spot at the back of the lodge.

"Is there a stone?" Gilbert asked.

I felt through the sage and found one. "Yes".

I thanked everyone who was in the lodge for their prayers and help during the ceremony, but...

Doubt crowded my mind. The stone could have easily been placed in the nest by Gilbert or his helper who sat near the door. They both were within easy reach of the nest. There was no proof that this stone came from outside the human realm. In fact the stone wasn't even unusual for the area outside of the lodge. I was able to go out and find many like it after I left the lodge.

To make the situation worse Gilbert took me aside afterwards and said, "The Tunkashilas say you need 2 nights on the hill and two nights of Yuwipi to be healed."

I finally asked why.

"It has to do with your faith".

It was true that I had lost my trust in the process. Even in my first Yuwipi I had my doubts about what had happened and here my doubt was strong. There was no foundation for my faith so it wavered.

Lack of faith had always been my trouble and it was obvious that no miracles were coming my way to help my belief. I drove away dejected with the promise of Gilbert getting back together with me that summer.

Gilbert stopped by our house in Tucson a few weeks later and we did a pipe ceremony in my living room. I had been honored with the gift of a Canupa, or sacred pipe, by Gilbert and he taught me how to properly hold a ceremony. Though I had used the pipe in prayer before, this was the first time I filled the pipe with the proper atmosphere as Gilbert played the drum and sang the pipe filling song. After the ceremony Gilbert gifted me with another stone already properly wrapped and made into a necklace. These stones, it was said, were often found in the ceremony room after the spirits left. All were collected and properly cared for by Gilbert. He gave them out occasionally to protect and encourage people.

The following July I headed for Idaho at the invitation of Gilbert. He was working outside of Boise and said he had the perfect spot for my vision quest and Yuwipi. He said "Come up here and we will finish you up".

I took the time off of work and drove north. When I got there Gilbert had decided that he didn't like the arrangement he had and was going back to South Dakota. His brother wouldn't bring out the family motor home so he imposed on me to help him out. He said we then could do my ceremony back at his place in South Dakota.

To some degree I liked the idea of doing the ceremony in that familiar place but I was put off by the financial burden of renting a car big enough for six members of Gilbert's family to ride in. None the less, I did it.

After returning to South Dakota and recuperating from the straight through drive. I prepared for my ceremony. Gilbert's old apprentice, Tony, was there to help and that was good for me. We gathered sage, the sacred herb, and rocks and wood. I tended the rocks for the sweat lodge and made double the amount of prayer ties so that we could do a double ceremony to get caught up. I ran out of time to prepare the meal so Gilbert's wife helped out.

The ceremony took place very late and Gilbert's mother said that the spirits we needed weren't going to be available after midnight to help us. Gilbert said nothing but the ceremony was sorely lacking. It reminded me of the first Yuwipi I had attended when the man didn't want to do what was required of him by the spirits.

Afterward Gilbert told me that I had a temporary healing and that by mid-October I needed to return to do either a 4 day sun dance or the 2 nights of vision quest and 2 nights of ceremony. I was thrilled. If what he said was true then I'd be medication free for now and I'd do whatever it took to return by October to really finish up and make it permanent. I took off that night and drove about 50 miles to a highway rest stop and slept.

When I woke up I didn't check my blood sugar. I didn't want to tempt fate and I felt no symptoms. A couple of hours later when I entered Wyoming I felt the symptoms of high blood sugar. I checked it at a rest stop and it was dangerously high. I called Gilbert. He said to call him back in one hour and he'd check to see what was going on. I believed that he was going to talk to the Tunkashilas in ceremony to find out why I had symptoms. I continued to drive assuming the answer would be something fixable but the answer led me away from Gilbert's path.

Gilbert said it was my lack of faith and my lack of belief that caused the change. "You will have to return to 'finish up' but all should have worked." I could attribute the other failures on my lack of faith but this time I was told I was healed and it wasn't true and I had great confidence that it was fact but it didn't hold. I could have turned around and spent several more days finishing up but I kept on going.

As I pondered the events of the past several days I thought of the fact that I had driven through Rapid City earlier that day but deliberately had not called or visited my friend Jerry. I knew what his reaction to all of this medicine man stuff would be and I didn't want to hear it. So I, who was rarely up that way, drove back to Tucson without seeing my friend. Looking back, I see signs of furtive movement.

Intertwined with the time I spent with Gilbert and seeking out the Lakota way Jerry would interject his opinion. We would have long conversations on the phone about belief and faith and he would ask me questions on how my search was progressing. I enjoyed the talks and debates but I was unnerved by the fact that he could always ask me a question that I couldn't answer about my faith. When I went to find the answer I never found one that made sense to me logically. To make things worse I often could talk to two different people with the same belief system and find answers to foundational questions to be in complete opposition. When I was able to call Jerry on the same sort of thing in Christianity he pointed to the Bible, the rulebook, and said even if someone claims to be a Christian if what they teach is opposed to the Bible then they are wrong. I didn't admit it to him at the time, but I liked that there was a standard that could be consulted in time of doubt on the essential items of the faith.

I started to see more and more that made sense about Jerry's faith but in my head I would have to give up my outdoor search if I went that way so I didn't. (If you ask me now why I thought that was true, I wouldn't be able to give you a logical answer. Was it someone's attempt at camouflage?) I finally decided if I was going to disagree with this faith I needed to study it more to know why I disagreed. During my discussions with Jerry he noticed that I had a solid foundation of the Bible already. I had never realized how much of the teachings of my youth had stayed with me.

I found myself sitting in my medicine circle in my back yard doing my pipe ceremony and praying for truth without knowing who I was praying to.

I was having a talk with a co-worker during my quest and told her of the trouble I was having knowing about God and who I was talking to when I prayed. She was not a strong believer in any particular faith, as far as I could tell, but she gave me a piece of advice that was to be a turning point in my search.

She said, "Randy, you have to have the faith that if God wants you to know who He is He will give you the information you need once you ask Him."

That struck me as very logical. My faith would not be in a God but in finding an answer if I sought it diligently. That night I put down my pipe and asked my questions about God without props. It was the first time I used the request mentioned in chapter nine. "God", I said, "Creator of all things I seek the truth about you. Please reveal yourself to me in a way that I will understand."

It took several months for anything that I could decipher to come to me and my lack of patience frustrated my efforts but I finally got an answer that made sense. I came across a book that knocked me over the fence I was straddling. It was written by an investigative reporter who asked the hard questions of Christianity and recorded the answers given to him by scientists and scholars of the Christian world. With an open mind I couldn't refute much of what I read on those pages. I chose Christ at that point. I knew that not all of my questions were answered yet, but Pascal's Wager came to my mind. If I was wrong on this choice the worst that would happen is that I'd be sent back to the starting point again. This decision lead me to an on going process of looking for gaps in the Christian faith and seeing if the teachings of the faith filled them in. As with the other avenues I had traveled down, I knew I would be disappointed if I found those irreparable gaps. Since I started down this path I have not been disappointed.

I hear some saying "Oh, come on!"

Others are saying "Tell me the title of that book!"*

The fact of the matter is that my epiphany will not be your epiphany. The book that tipped the scales for me has been a gift from me to others without the effect I had hoped for from the reader. I don't think it a coincidence that I asked for the answer to come to me in a language that could understand. I believe that all seekers, if they really want the truth, will get an answer that they can wrap their own brain around. And if that seeker doesn't want to experience the truth he will get that answer as well. I think how quickly I had an answer to my prayer on Bear Butte and how long I ignored it. It wasn't the truth I wanted to hear. It wasn't the truth that fit into what I wanted to happen.

My rule book says this about truth; seek and you will find it. Those may seem like empty words to you, but to me they are a promise fulfilled. When I first applied them to my quest I was frustrated because of my impatience. When I did a deeper search into the meaning of that line from the original text, I found that not only was one to seek, but one was to keep seeking. I have misread information in my quest, but I find if I stay on the path, my answers come. They come when I am ready to understand and in a language that makes sense to me. I still get answers that I wish I didn't have to believe, but that is my payment in this wager. Christianity offers the most believable reward in the realm of big payoffs.

*The Case for Christ by Lee Strobel

11.

MY TRUTH

You can use the process outlined in this book and never come to the conclusion I have. I think it is the only one that answers all of the hard questions that plagued me during my quest, and as we discovered, all faiths can not be reconciled with one another. So either Jesus is God as the Christian faith claims or he is not as many other faiths contend. Both can't be true. If you have looked into the option and have discarded it, I hope you will reconsider.

One of the things that drew me into the possibility of exploring Christianity was the way I turned from it irrationally. When I looked at that with my law enforcement eye, I immediately saw a furtive movement scenario. When Christianity was presented to me I ran hard the other way but as I was making ground away from the threat I looked around and wondered why I ran.

I was annoyed by the way some Christians presented themselves and I hated their holier-than-thou attitude. As I sat back and watched my, and others, behavior I realized that the reaction was greater than the annoyance allowed for.

After years of being offended by the line "there is only one way to God" I started to notice some things. Whenever I was with a group of people who discussed their spiritual beliefs, there seemed to only be an offense when someone confessed a Christian faith. I saw people who followed the spiritual ways of the Hindu, the Buddhist, the Native American and even the Jew, which is the foundation of the Christian faith, welcomed into the conversation. When someone said "I am a Christian", though, the walls went up and people rolled their eyes. It was all right to say that you believed in God but not all right to say that you believed in Jesus Christ as God. This intrigued me both from the watching and the experiencing point of view. I saw the evidence of furtive movement, of someone trying to hide or avoid something. I just didn't know whom. Or what. So I watched and waited. I didn't believe this religion had merit but I was still interested in how the scene was playing out. The part that interested me was that the people involved were expressing points of view that could not be reconciled with each other but, in the name of tolerance, ignored that fact. As stated before, the doctrine of the Hindu clashes with that of the Buddhist. By the standards of logic they should be open to hearing each other but if one way is followed you have to say that the other is wrong. You can and should be tolerant of other people's point of view but you can't logically say it has the same merit as your truth; otherwise your truth is empty.

What I observed, as mentioned in chapter 8, was a consistent acceptance of everything but the most vile (Satanism with blood sacrifices) or the doctrine of Christ. Since I knew that the teachings of the man Jesus were ones of love and acceptance, I was intrigued by the dichotomy. It seemed that the teachings of love were accepted and that the man Jesus was a fine teacher, but when it came to these Christian zealots saying that this was the only way then everyone backed off. This claim to be an exclusive route to God could not hold true because no loving God would give us such limits. All dedicated believers, no matter what the belief, should get the same devotion from this all-loving God without restriction.

This leads to the well known argument about the claims of Jesus. Muslims call him a great prophet, Hindus say that he was an avatar; the Jews say he was a great Rabbi but that all conflicts with the fact that Jesus claimed to be God Himself. Again either he was or he wasn't. So that makes him a liar, crazy or God. The first two make the other faiths claims about him absurd. How can we say that he is a great anything if he is loony enough to believe he is God? So it looked to me that in order to write off the possibility of that conclusion, Jesus was accepted into other faiths in a way that allowed control of the outcome. Logic says that doesn't work. He is either who he says he is or we have to discount him completely. Most faiths don't do either.

The part that struck me was that people were taking what they wanted from the works of Jesus and leaving the stuff they didn't like behind. As we discussed in chapter 3, they weren't playing by the rules. In my mind you can't have it both ways. Either Christ was who he said he was or not. He wasn't a great teacher if he lied to us, yet many, for comforts sake, put him in that box by saying that was all he was.

Another thing that struck me was why would a person, who was trying to gain a following, give such a restrictive way for success? If I wanted acceptance I would be sure that you could do most of what you wanted to do. The restrictions put on us by the God of the Bible are some of the things that lead people to call Christians zealots, prudes and fanatics. So if what Christ said was true, and logic dictates that we want at least some of it to be true or we wouldn't give him any credit at all, and if I, as the instigator of this furtive movement, wanted to counter a truth with such limitations what better tactic than to offer any other, more broad and accepting spiritual solution. We all look for acceptance, even when we do things with questionable integrity. It made sense to me that my unfounded repulsion to Christians was somehow magnified beyond my actual connection with the people involved.

The question that continued to haunt me was why? Why, with this religion and only with this one was I feeling tugged away when I was at least open to hearing the concepts of the others without offense? Even if I didn't believe in the concept I remained open. I saw internal furtive movement at work and felt that I needed to stick around and see what it was trying to hide.

What I found, and what I would encourage you to look at, is the accuracy of the Christian belief system.

It was overwhelming for me to look at the thickness of the Bible and the small font of the words and figure that I would ever get the opportunity to actually read the rulebook. If I couldn't read it I was never going to be able to prove it right or wrong so I thought I might as well just forget it. That seemed like more furtive movement. So I looked into what the Bible was and what it was about.

As mentioned in chapter 8, the Bible is 66 books written over the course of 1500 years by over 40 authors. That in itself is not extremely impressive but the fact that it is internally consistent is. The purpose of all those books is to show the need for, and the eventual arrival of, the Messiah. An over simplification would be that the Old Testament reveals how we got here and what was expected of us. It also shows that we, on our own are not capable of fulfilling those requirements. As people with a free will we mess up. We want to do what is right but still fall down on the job. God created us to have a relationship with Him but he can't be in the presence of our indiscretions. He leads us to a way to correct that. He could have just created us to love him unconditionally but programmed love is not real love. The gift of free will is both a blessing and a curse to both the creator and the receiver.

So since we have the will to choose and we have the tendency to choose poorly, God sent a solution. The New Testament gives the details of this plan. The coming of the Messiah is foretold in detail in the Old Testament and is fulfilled in the New. Keep in mind the number of authors and the period of time taken to do all of this precludes the possibility of a well planned conspiracy. If I wrote a book that I claimed to be a rulebook of God I could plot twist my way from front to back and have it all turn out the way I needed it to in order to gain followers. If I had made up the end that I wanted, you will worship me and give me all your money, then I could write the beginning to line up with that result. Every novel ever written uses that formula. The difference with the Bible is that the things that were written that foretell the future were written years, even centuries, before the specific event occurred. When the event does occur it occurs with all of the details in place. Prophecy is not prophecy unless it is 100% accurate. The difference between the psychic hotline and the predictions of the Bible are that one is vague and occasionally right and the other is 100% right 100% of the time.

Spiritual belief does not have to be complicated. In fact I believe that the critical elements are meant to be easy to understand. We can ponder various themes for the rest of our days but the basics need to be articulated briefly, concisely, and believably with merit to anyone with an open mind who is willing to listen. The other requirement is that even in its simplicity when questions arise the details have to be deep enough that objections can be logically answered by the doctrine of the belief.

I do work for a company that markets a certain product. The process for doing the work successfully has been designed and is laid out for every new associate. The history of the company shows that anyone doing the work as laid out by the proven plan has success in accordance with the time they put in. If someone comes to the company and tries to change the system, usually by complicating it, they start to notice the properties of diminishing returns.

The same is true for understanding God. The basics are already laid out and the process is easy to follow. We tend to run into trouble when we try to alter the plan either because we can't stand that it is so easy or because we don't like the fact that we have to follow a simple or restrictive plan. We tend to want to make sure that we feel like we have the protection of a god and can still do what ever we want without restriction.

So the simplicity is in the message and the difficulty is in the rules of engagement. I can believe that Jesus died for me, but I can't as easily accept my obligation in that relationship.

I think this is where we, as people, moved away from God. There are those who can't see God's presence in life for various reasons and those who see that God has to exist but try to understand Him in completely human terms. It has to be fair to say that if something beyond our understanding of existence created the world and put us here there are going to be things, maybe many things, about the rules that we won't understand. We perceive our lives based on rules and laws that we "discover" and then define with our minds. If God is omniscient, omnipresent, etc., there are going to be things that He doesn't need to let us in on that are common place in His world.

Think of an illusionist. He may be able to perform tricks and acts of slight-of-hand that baffle the non-illusionist. Yet once you know the trick it becomes painfully apparent. This in no way implies that the idea of God is an illusion but there will always be things beyond our grasp when we try to put it all together. We are not omniscient. The great joy and the great trial of having such a profound, searching mind is that we assume that all things are knowable and either get frustrated, or just write off anything that we can't explain as voodoo.

I have long been fascinated by the ability of science fiction writers to come up with worlds and gadgets that are so far out there during the time of the writer only to have a future scientist create the technology to make such things doable. As an example look at what Jules Vern did with his literature and how much of that we live with now day to day.

If creative, intelligent people can manufacture such scenarios that stun and amaze us how much more simple would it be for an all powerful God?

The simplicity of Christianity is this: God created us for his great pleasure and for communion. We weren't capable of being perfect so we needed a way, brought about by God, to cover us in our imperfection. Remember free will still has to be a factor. The solution was that God came to earth as a human to live the perfect life and then was sacrificed to atone for our imperfections. The sacrifice was done in the tradition of the Jewish law so that it would be understood by the culture within which it occurred and it was predicted in detail 500 years before the mechanism of Jesus' death was invented.

The difficult part is we have to choose to believe that this happened. We aren't covered just because. We have to take that step of faith and say we believe in our hearts that it is so. The good news for this conversion is that evidence abounds. We can prove enough of what is in the Bible with math, logic, science and archeology to surmise the things we can't point at directly.

The simple part is that we don't have to be perfect. Jesus has already taken the hit for our faults on our behalf and he did so lovingly and by choice. The hard part is stepping up and allowing someone else to be in charge of our lives and giving up the need to be in complete control. We don't have to be perfect, we don't have to do 100 push ups but we do have to accept the atonement done on our behalf on the cross and admit that we can't be perfect.

If you can get enough information to do that you reap the benefit of Pascal's Wager.

As I think about all of the preparations for the Yuwipi ceremony and all of the time and effort required to make it happen I am reminded of a line from a song by the Righteous Brothers. They sang "The simplicity of God somehow escapes men". I pondered that line for many years after I first heard it. I sang the song because the power of the music moved me but I found no simplicity in my search for and practice of the things of God. In the Yuwipi ceremony I had to whittle cherry wood a specific way and save the shavings. I had to make 405 prayer ties to call the 405 stone spirits and then make 75 more for the altar and 50 more for the food area. I then had to make the 7 prayer flags to mark the sacred directions. I then had to ask for my healing in a very specific way because the healing would take place as I asked for not as I might need it. We can look at the religious ceremonies of many tribes, cultures and even within the Christian world and find a complexity that distracts from the actual communion with the underlying God. The ceremony becomes the important thing and my part in it is an integral part. If I mess up then God is not capable of overcoming my mistake. In this case God is not really sought out but it is the perfection of the ritual; the proof that I did my good works and now I will receive what is due me.

I have found that the simplicity of what God asks of us in the Christian tradition is easy enough, at least in principal, for anyone to do anywhere very quickly and effectively.

We don't have to climb Bear Butte, we don't have to get into an altered state of awareness, and we don't have to face a certain direction or pray incessantly. All you have to do is this. Accept that there is only one God, that he came to earth as a man to live the perfect life in our place because we are not able to be perfect, he died on the cross as a sacrifice to atone for our imperfections and he rose from the dead on the third day in part as a sign of our future resurrection. If we can and will truly accept that, we will be forever forgiven. That is all.

I did say something about simplicity before didn't I? Remember that the difficulty arises when we resist this because of our desire to be in control, at least that's where my resistance came from. Even if you can't get your right brain to wrap around that concept God has promised to send you the people, circumstance or resources to convince you if you will diligently search for the truth. (Consider the fact that you are reading *this* book at *this* time in your quest.)

If you follow the concepts of this book will it lead to the Christian faith? That depends on your interpretation of the material you gather. I know what I am about to write will seem narrow and offend some but I believe that the Christian faith is the only one that is ultimately lead to by this process.

We can't get around presupposition. I will present my opinion on Christianity with certain presuppositions in place and you will review and make your judgments about what I present with yours. To be fair to the quest and to each other, we both have to be open to the possibility that the other has valid information to be considered.

Presupposition, used correctly, can be a good thing to keep you safe while exploring uncharted territory. It becomes a liability if we adhere to it so tightly that we don't let in any new information. This tends to happen when the information is in conflict with what we believe. As we get closer to the truth the information we take in has to make sense and be provable. Sooner or later you will see bad logic coming at you and you will be able to quickly discard it. Just don't discard it without putting it through the full process.

So what is the truth? That takes time to figure out. But remember that it is the tendency of most people to decide what it is then only apply the things that keep it alive to their process. You have to start somewhere (your presupposition) then openly add or subtract as logical thought prevails. If truth exists then so must ultimate truth. Remember the candy bar scenario (a list of truths don't necessarily add up to the whole truth) and don't stop researching until all the sources are exhausted. This doesn't have to be overwhelming research. There is nothing wrong with plinking away until you get to the end of a route. Just keep in mind that the Who you ask is equally as important. If not more important, as the what you ask. Christianity is the only world religion that has a preponderance of historical evidence. The places and times chronicled in the Bible (including the Jewish foundation of this faith found in the Old Testament) are solidly represented in the archeological record. Over the years many claims were made that certain people or places didn't exist but nearly all of them have been proven through the work of the archeological spade.

No matter which faith you choose to follow it is fair to say that you shouldn't judge a philosophy by its abuses. If I claim to be a Christian but act un-Christ like that doesn't impeach Christ's message, just mine. If I do as Christ commanded and that impeaches something else that he commanded, I then have to question the veracity of the belief system.

Christ's claims were definitive. He claimed to be God. This by itself isn't much evidence. I could claim to be a kumquat and not convince too many people. Christ claims are definitive and fully predicted long before He came on the scene.

The Baker Encyclopedia of Christian Apologetics by Norman L. Geisler lists the following 16 predictions, made centuries in advance, for evidence that Jesus was the coming Messiah. (There are more than these but these are enough to make the point).

1) Born of a woman (Genesis 3:15; Galatians 4:4).
2) Born of a virgin (Isaiah 7:14; Matthew 1:21).
3) Cut off (would die) 483 years after the declaration to reconstruct the temple in 444 B.C. (Daniel 9:24. This was fulfilled to the year. See Hoehner, 115-38).
4) The seed of Abraham (Genesis 12:1-3 and 22:18; Matthew 1:1 and Galatians 3:16).
5) Of the tribe of Judah (Genesis 49:10; Luke 3:23, 33 and Hebrews 7:14).
6) A descendant of David (2 Samuel 7:12; Matthew 1:1).
7) Born in Bethlehem (Micah 5:2; Matthew 2:1 and Luke 2:4-7).
8) Anointed by the Holy Spirit (Isaiah 11:2 and Matthew 3:16-17).
9) Heralded by a messenger (Isaiah 40:3 and Malachi 3:1; Matthew 3:1-2).

10) A worker of miracles (Isaiah 35:5-6; Matthew 9:35).

11) Cleanser of the temple (Malachi 3:1; Matthew21:12).

12) Rejected by Jews (Psalms 118:22; 1 Peter 2:7).

13) Die a humiliating death (Psalms 22 and Isaiah 53; Matthew 27:3) His death would involve: enduring rejection by his own people (Isaiah 53:3; John 1:10-11; 7:5, 48). Standing silence (sic) before his accusers (Isaiah 53:7; Matthew 27:12-19). Being mocked (Psalms 27:-8; Matthew 27:31). Having hands and feet pierced (Psalms 22:16; Luke23:33). Being crucified with thieves (Isaiah 53:12; Mark 15:27-28). Praying for his persecutors (Isaiah 53:12; Luke 23:34). The piercing of his side (Zechariah 12:10; John 19:34). Burial in a rich mans tomb (Isaiah 53:9; Matthew 27:57-60). The casting of lots for his garments (Psalms 22:18; John 19:23-24). 14) Being raised from the dead (Psalms 2:7 and 16:10; Acts 2:31 and Mark 16:6).

15) Ascending into heaven (Psalms 68:18; Acts 1:9).

16) Sitting at the right hand of God (Psalms 110:1; Hebrews 1:3).

The article states "Even the most liberal critics admit that the prophetic books were completed 400 years before Christ and the Book of Daniel no later than 165 B.C. There is good evidence to date these books much earlier..."

If we go with the laws of mathematical probability it is so unlikely as to be impossible for one man to fulfill all of these prophecies and not be who the prophets claimed Him to be. The prophets, and He Himself, claimed that He is God.

I take it very seriously when I read that Jesus said "I am the way, the truth and the life. No one comes to the Father except through me" (John 14:6). This means that the opportunity we have to be with God hinges on this choice. We don't have to take it but the reason I sat down to write this book was so that you would have enough information to make your choice a conscious one. If that offends, please understand that according to the rulebook I follow I am obligated to tell you about this "with gentleness and respect" (1 Peter 3:15). I do that because I have found that the rulebook of Christianity has the characteristics that fulfill the logic and reason my mind requires to follow this path.

If we are to play by the rules those rules have to be internally and eternally consistent. When I play made up games with my youngest son he will often change the rules as new ideas occur to him. It's fun to watch him ponder the game and how to make it work for him but I would never want to follow a leader who changed the definitive rules. An all knowing God has a plan already set out and has no reason to change the program. If He did we could never know what to do or if what we are doing is right. I look to the rulebook to see if my human leaders are leading well and to see if I am doing what is expected of me. When those rules are constant I know that any alteration has come from me and I get to choose whether or not to continue down that path. I have not found an instance where the Bible is inconsistent. In fact, as noted in the list above, throughout all the centuries it was being produced it held a constant theme (that we can't follow the laws set for us by God) and it fulfilled that theme (that Christ must come to be our salvation). I don't find that consistency in the other rulebooks I have searched through. In fact, not only does the Bible have that consistency but there is evidence outside of the Bible that backs up its historic claims. It is one thing for someone to make a claim; it is quite another when people who have no gain in the matter back up that claim. Both happen for the Bible.

When it comes to contrast in our quest, the claims of Christ are unique. Jesus is the only founder of a world religion that claimed to be God. If He is God, He would know that, and lying would be impossible. We have shown, though, that because of contrast we know that He could be lying because both truth and falsehood exist. But contrast has to be taken within the worldview as well. In the message of the faith there should not be any contrast. Remember; don't judge a philosophy by its abuses. But if the founders of a world religion approve of both the Black view and the White view, then we have to consider that there is unhealthy contrast in the faith. If you don't believe what I believe we both can't be right. I can't offer both black and white and expect to be taken seriously.

For some the claims of Christ seem too far fetched. I say, when taken in context of the whole story it fits well with logical thought. Since there can't be more that one ultimate truth, we have to chose the one that answers all of the criteria to be convincing, even in the things that seem out of reach. We can find things in Christianity that fit into that out of reach classification but taken in the context of the whole, and with the corroborating evidence outside the faith, we have the most documented provable faith in all of the world religions.

There are many who can write a book, claim it is from God and start a religion. Just like writing a novel, the author knows how it will come out so, they can make anything fit within reason. It is common that one person goes out, has a vision or a meeting with an angel and comes back with a new worldview. I even think that most of those who have done this received their inspiration from a source that they believed to be angelic or divine. But what is more likely to be believable? One person, claiming something that no one else has seen coming back to claim that they had a vision from God with no solid outside corroboration or many people over the course of many centuries experiencing the same sort of information, making precise future predictions that so far have been 100% accurate. Coupled with this there is historical evidence found by archeologists, who have no interest in the outcome, that support the facts written and writings from other faiths that point to the alleged happenings of the faith in question.

If you like the first way, then try this. I sought enlightenment, I prayed and God told me to believe in Christ. Now you must do the same.

If you like the second option this will be your route. Look deeply into my claims of Christ and the early church and see if logic and evidence support it. In fact you should do this with whatever you intend to follow in your quest. Just keep an open mind and heart during the search. Your job is to prove your choice right or prove it wrong. Use the scientific method here when you can.

In that open-mindedness you have to remember to consider the source. Who you are asking for the information? This is where you have to keep in mind the concepts of who do I ask and spiritual camouflage. If you ask someone who wants to lead you away from the truth your course will be altered. Even so, if that is the case, and your open heart and mind are working, alarms will go off. If you seek the truths of a false doctrine and ask the founder of that doctrine about those truths, most of the time he will be able to answer your questions to your satisfaction. You have the obligation to double check the veracity of that information.

I know that God will answer your prayers if you are truly searching with an open heart and mind even if you ask in a roundabout way. The trouble arises when your heart wants a different answer than the truth. There are plenty of folks out there who will tell you what you want to hear and keep you nudged off the path to the narrow gate. The ones concentrating on misleading you aren't dressed in black. If they are doing their jobs well they look just like the one you want to get your information from. How do you tell if the information is good? Double check it against the rulebook and double check the rulebook against itself and your internal moral compass. If it all doesn't align do some more digging.

Prophecies of the Bible include some very pointed information on folks being deceived by those posing as "Angels of light" and of the many false teachings that would come "to deceive even the elect". As more and more belief systems and variations of Christianity surface, those teachings with some truth intertwined, I see another of the things I admire about the Bible coming to pass. 100% accuracy in its predictions.

If Christianity is right, and I know it is, how would someone who wanted to steer people away from the teaching do it? How could I, as minister of the bad guys, prevent people from taking this world-view seriously?

God was deliberate in laying out the facts in such a way that you still have the freedom to choose. I, as the bad guy, see that as a chink in His armor. I can put doubt in your head based on that free will. In fact the gate is so narrow that leads to salvation that I can use nearly anything to sway you. Even some of the teachings of Jesus himself! In fact let's start with this: "If God is all powerful and all knowing why does he make it so hard for you to understand this? He must not exist! At least not in the narrow way that is presented by those puritans".

My job is to nudge you off the route to the narrow gate. Going back to a biking scenario, if you were riding headlong down a hill on a difficult path aiming toward a narrow gate (which is always open, by the way) and I could nudge you, just a little, your outcome would be off the path. Maybe I succeed early and you lose momentum and decide to seek an easier path. Maybe I reach you late and you miss the opening at full speed and become a messy spot on the wall. I don't care which as long as you miss the gate. (I have to admit, though the messy spot is the fun way for me, as the minister of the bad guys).

One of the things that kept me on this path was the furtive movement sensation of how easy it was for the other side. All religions have some shared basic principals and variations that can be based on them: If you just live a good life all will be fine. If you mess up this life you will have another in which to make it up. A loving god would never send anyone to hell so don't worry, everyone goes to heaven. But if you come back to Matthew 7:14 "Because narrow is the gate and difficult the way which leads to life, and there are few who will find it.", we come to a disturbing prophecy: Many will choose the wrong way.

As the bad guy I am already assured a certain victory. Many will follow me, I just don't know who. It is easier and more fun for us to do as we please as opposed to living by some narrow set of rules. We figure that as long as I am good to my mother and kind to strangers I can justify stealing from the office supply closet. I'm a good guy and the company has plenty of money so they won't miss this stuff. Besides, I work hard and they don't pay me enough anyway. The slippery slope begins and it becomes easier and easier to justify improper behavior and harder and harder to seek out someone or something that will require us to admit our faults and help us to not repeat them.

My job as the bad guy is so simple I can't stand it! I hope they pull out that word sinner when they catch you "borrowing" pens and copy paper. I can make you so indignant about the accusation that you will never even look up what the word sin means. I can make you rationalize your behavior based on your characterization of them.

God's choice was to plant in everyone the need for this quest. Romans 1:20 states, "For since the creation of the world God's invisible qualities- his eternal power and divine nature- have been clearly seen, being understood from what has been made, so that men are without excuse."

And Psalms 19:1-4 states, "The heavens declare the glory of God; the skies proclaim the work of His hands. Day after day they pour forth speech; night after night they display knowledge. There is no speech or language where their voice is not heard. Their voice goes out into all the earth, their words to the end of the world."

These passages show that a way to know the truth about God is placed in us upon our creation and the natural world that we live in speaks to us daily about the existence of God. We can choose to ignore it, but it is there for all to see and use.

In my quest I struggled because I thought I'd have to give up my outdoor life if I accepted this Christian thing. The psalmist tells me otherwise. I knew from childhood that I saw God in nature. The camouflage master helped me to believe that I wanted to avoid the quest for Christ by placing the fear in my mind that I would have to lose something that I loved. There is no logic in that idea yet I held on to it for years and years.

"Good camo".

That camouflage seems to be solidly in place when we try to reconcile the Bible with science. There are those who say that the Bible is allegory and mythological and certainly shouldn't be taken literally. Science, they say, is well, science and can't mesh with religion and God. Most today don't even know that many of the early founders of scientific method and laws were devout people of faith. When I was searching for the truth I certainly saw the effects of science in nature. I also heard the call of God there. I needed to find a connection between the two worlds since it made sense that, if created, they had to have the same source.

Norman Geisler points out in an article on "Science and the Bible" that when we look at science we find that it is constantly changing. New information comes along and old theories have to be altered or discarded. There is also fallible interpretation of the infallible word of God. Basically truth exists but we, as imperfect humans, misinterpret it. Whether it is scientific or Biblical. So to assume that there are scientific errors in the Bible we have to first assume that

1) "Something is known for certain to be a scientific fact, and

2) it conflicts with an interpretation of Scripture that is beyond all doubt".

The fact is that the Bible was written during a time of scientific ignorance yet it holds truths that are verified by science. A partial list of those truths, as outlined by Geisler is:

1) The universe had a beginning. Both the first line of the bible and the Big Bang Theory agree to this.

2) Matter can neither be created nor destroyed. So states the First Law of Thermodynamics and Genesis 2:2 where it states that God completed the creation of the universe and then rested.

3) According to the second law of thermodynamics the useable energy in the universe is running down. This is confirmed by Psalms 102:25-27 "In the beginning you laid the foundations of the earth, and the heavens are the work of your hand. They will perish but you remain; like clothing you will change them and they will be discarded."

4) Genesis 2:7 states "The Lord God formed the man from the dust of the ground and breathed into his nostrils the breath of life, and the man became a living being." According to science "the constituent elements of the human body are the same as those found in the earth." (Geisler, The Baker Encyclopedia of Christian Apologetics pg 692-693)

And on it goes. That correlation between two alleged irreconcilable sources actually points to the truth that I wanted to know.

The Bible has numerous examples of evidence outside of itself that point to its truths. Historical accounts of the times and circumstances of what is depicted in the Bible give credence to the information given in the Bible. This circumstantial evidence is not enough when it stands by itself but coupled with the rest of the information it makes a powerful case for the Truth of the Bible. And as we saw with Pascal's Wager it is wise to bet on only one truth.

Remember you have the right to reject all of this, but if that is the way you are leaning consider the process outlined in this book again and see if it doesn't make sense. If not my conclusion at least the process I used to arrive at that conclusion. No one ever said that the quest for spiritual truth was going to be easy. But if you find the truth (and the truth is the truth no matter what you believe) "...the truth shall set you free".

12.

EPILOUGE

In the Quest for Spiritual Truth how can we discern the real truth coming from the real God when it is presented to us? We have to trust our sources of back up information. The Bible was written by a host of people over centuries of time yet it hasn't yet missed one aspect of one of the predictions it has made. That is impressive. The same can not be said for any other rulebook of any other world religion. That speaks volumes.

If you send out a prayer and get back an answer that you are uncertain about you need to check it against the rule book that you follow. The answers will correspond with the truths contained within. If you can trust your rulebook then all is well. If there is doubt of the trustworthiness of your rulebook then continue your quest.

In the beginning this whole thing can be confusing and frustrating but to know the truth is worth it. There are those, both within your circle of influence and outside the physical world that would like to see you fail for their own selfish reasons. So expect some conflict as you get closer to the truth. You may be feeling some now. Keep in mind also that there are those both within and outside this physical world that would love to see you succeed in this quest. I am one of them, God is another.

This isn't meant to be a rubbing of the magic lamp and getting all the knowledge you want all at once sort of exercise. But I can guarantee that if you are truly seeking the truth, the truth will find you. Don't stop seeking. In fact, when it gets hard consider it may be because you are getting close and something is trying to frustrate you so you will just back away. I find encouragement in those moments and keep plugging away.

The question that comes up often by this point is "If Christianity is the only way why is there so much regular opposition to the faith?"

The short answer is there is a dark side out there that doesn't want anyone to know this stuff. Did you notice repulsion to that last comment? Did you ever wonder how so many people can believe in Guardian Angels, as seen by the bumper stickers on the subject, but no one ever talks about the angels who are against us? If a good angel can be sitting with me for protection then a bad one could be there, for other reasons, as well. 2 Corinthians 11:14 says "And no wonder! For Satan himself transforms himself into an angel of light. Therefore, it is no great thing if his ministers also transform themselves into ministers of righteousness, whose end shall be according to their works."

That is the camouflage that allows people to follow the wrong philosophy.

There are also many people who don't want what they feel are the restrictions that will be required by the Christian belief. It is easier for us as ego driven, independent minded humans to say, "Stand back. I can take care of myself. And when I do my reward will be that I can do what I want when I want to. If I join up with that Christian crowd I'll have to stop _____ and that isn't going to happen." You fill in the blank. Remember I thought I had to give up outdoor education!

The thing to keep in mind is that the Bible, which hasn't been wrong yet, says all of us will live forever. You and I are now eternal beings. But we have a choice to make and there are grand rewards or severe consequences for our choice. One is eternity with God the other is eternity without God. Both are forever without an option to change. The promise is that in the end we will all know the truth, finally, but it is in the here and now that we chose our eternal outcome. The more I learn about this process the more that concerns me. All I ask is that you look into what this means.

Why would a loving God do that to anyone? Because without freewill to chose we are nothing but robots and robots don't offer real love. We either choose to love or choose to ignore but we have knowledge of what the outcome will be and still have the right to choose.

In the movie "Indiana Jones and the Last Crusade" there is a scene where Jones and his arch enemy have both entered a chamber where the Holy Grail is supposed to be. The bad guy wants to possess it to gain eternal life. Jones wants it to save the life of his father who was shot by the bad guy. The room is guarded by an old man who has been there for centuries and watches over several dozen cups, any of which could be the sought after chalice. The bad guy pushes Jones aside and chooses a cup and drinks from it to gain that eternal life. He, of course, starts to shake and his face distorts and ultimately he dies a horrible death. The old man in the room looks at Jones and says "He chose poorly". My purpose in writing this book is so that you will have a process so you will not choose poorly.

You may ask, "Why should I believe anything that is in this book?" My answer, which I hope is obvious by now, is that you shouldn't just believe it. You need to do some checking- remember to always double check your sources. You need to ponder what has been written here and back it up or tear it down. In that process please keep an open heart and an objective point of view. Blind faith is not required nor requested. Matthew 12:30 says "And you shall love the lord your God with all your heart, with all your soul, with all your strength, *and with all your mind.*" You have a God given brain that gives you the ability to reason. Feel free to use it to find the logic in the process of faith.

I can safely say that I don't have all of the answers about my faith. I do, however, have the capacity to seek out the answers. So far I have been able to come up with logical, reasonable, believable answers to all of my questions. That's a comfort. I don't have to rationalize to get my belief system to work. Christianity works in an understandable way with or without me.

My final question is why did you read this book? What made you pick it up? Was it the title, a recommendation from a friend, did it happen to be sitting in the table at the doctor's office? I believe, and I hope you will consider the possibility, that it was a divine appointment. I don't believe in coincidences so we have met on these pages for reasons beyond you and me.

So I ask you to consider the options presented here openly and fairly. Check out the things you doubt. Research the things that resonate. Look through the list of suggested reading and pick up a book to move you toward the answer that you can live with. I know why I wrote this book. I respectfully ask you to keep studying and researching until you know for sure why you read it.

You are in my prayers.

Finally, if you believe that what I have presented is the way to go, all that is required of you is to ask for Christ to come into your life. That is when the education really begins! The process to start this relationship is easy; just send out a heartfelt prayer like the following:

Dear Heavenly Father,
I confess that I have sinned,
and I know my sin separates me from you.
I also know that I can be forgiven
by the death of Jesus upon the cross.
So I turn from my sin,
and I invite you into my life
that I may live for you.
I pray this in the name of Jesus,
Amen.

If you prayed this from your heart, even if you have reasonable doubt, your life will have changed. You will not necessarily have a carefree life but you will have a purpose beyond our ordinary existence. I'm excited for you. Please drop me a line if I can a help. Help@willowriverwilderness.com

FOR FURTHER STUDY:

Behe, Michael J. <u>Darwin's Black Box</u>. Touchstone/ Simon & Schuster Inc., 1996

Giesler, Norman L. <u>The Baker Encyclopedia of Christian Apologetics</u>. Baker Books, 1999

Hanegraff, Hank <u>The Face That Demonstrates the Farce of Evolution</u>. Word Publishing, 1998

Lewis, C. S. <u>Mere Christianity</u>. Touchstone/Simon & Schuster Inc., 1980

McDowell, Josh <u>The New Evidence That Demands A Verdict</u>. Thomas Nelson Inc., 1999

Pascal, Blaise <u>Mind On Fire</u>. Edited by James M. Houston Multnomah Press, 1989

Strobel, Lee <u>The Case For Christ</u>. Zondervan, 1998

Strobel, Lee The Case For A Creator. Zondervon, 2004

Toropov, Brandon & Buckles, Luke The Complete Idiot's Guide to World Religions. Alpha Publishing, 2002

Also include in your study any of the "Rule Books" used in the belief system of your choice.

Printed in the United States
89143LV00001B/67-75/A